200 YEARS
OF AMERICAN
FIREARMS

by JAMES E. SERVEN

edited by JOSEPH J. SCHROEDER, Jr.

Follett Publishing Company / Chicago

T-0599

Editorial Staff

Joseph J. Schroeder, Jr.
  Editor

Wanda Sahagian
  Production Manager

Mary MacDonald
  Art Director

James M. Triggs
  Cover Artist

Sheldon L. Factor
  Associate Publisher

ISBN 0-695-80599-1   Library of Congress Catalog Card #74-25251

A Dedication

The primary purpose of this book is not to eulogize the worthy patriots of the past but rather to emphasize some of the principles and activities that have assured our independence and progress for 200 years.

Our glorious heritage of liberty and enterprise was not born overnight; it is the result of the ingenuity, determination, hard work, suffering and sacrifice of many dedicated men and women. Not the least of these are the craftsmen who provided the weapons with which Americans have been able to win and preserve their freedoms.

It is hoped at this important milestone in our national existence we may rededicate ourselves to a diligent preservation of the fundamental principles which have given us such a rich heritage; and that the path of history may not be made less commendable by some who may attempt to change our way of life.

James E. Serven

Arms historian and author, James Serven.

Introduction

In the following pages noted arms expert and historian James Serven has done a remarkable job of reviewing the evolution of America's small arms. From the matchlock and occasional wheellock of the Pilgrims through the M16 rifle and compact double-action self-loading pistol of 1976, the new world's arms have always reflected the needs, inventive capabilities and spirit of a dynamic free people.

This review of more than two centuries of arms evolution is arranged in chronological order. To facilitate the reader's use of the book it has been arranged into more or less equal parts, each part highlighted by a period *(the colonies, the westward push)* or a war. Such divisions seemed logical, not only chronologically but because each such division usually reflected a changing role for America's firearms and created the impetus for another forward step in their evolution.

You'll find a lot of guns in these pages, some rare products of obscure makers and others well known to every American, not only the dedicated gun buff. This is a gun story, and guns have played a key role in bringing America from a few shaky settlements clinging precariously to the eastern seaboard to its present position as the world's leading nation. We've come a long way in the past two centuries plus, and done it as a free people in a democratic society. Despite those who abuse our freedoms, our constitutionally established right to enjoy the legitimate use of firearms for sport and personal protection has played a key part in our ability to become the world's leading nation of free people. Let us hope and pray the misguided intentions of those who fail to see this connection—and think somehow that repression of guns will miraculously change the irresponsible minority into law-abiding citizens—will not abrogate this key right of a free people!

Joseph Schroeder

Contents

CHAPTER ONE
Guns Come to America

ndian natives of the American continent first heard the sound of gunfire in the early 1500s when Spanish explorers led by such adventurous men as Cortes, Narvaez, De Soto, Coronado and Oñate explored Indian lands and named them "New Spain." The pyrotechnic qualities of those early guns —matchlocks and wheel-locks—savored of magic to the frightened Indians, and most soon were the victims of conquest.

It was not until a century later, however, that arms and armsmakers began to play a very substantial role in American life. This happened not in "New Spain" but far to the north-east in the colonies of "New England." Here the Massachusetts Bay Company, debarking almost a thousand settlers from a fleet of sailing ships in 1630, planted the artisan nucleus of what was to become a thriving American gunmaking trade.

While Jamestown had been established in 1607 and the Plymouth Colony in 1620, neither appeared to contain in those early years, any gunmaking capacity of the type that later spread out from Boston.

The first colonial gunmakers busied themselves with repairing the imported European weapons, and what few arms they did put together followed well-known European patterns. It is well to remember that at this point of our arms history soldiers sometimes wore armor, and the "hard hats" of those days were of steel and are known by such names as a *Salade, Barbute, Morion, Cabasset,* etc. Swords were a regular part of the military equipment.

A few crossbows were brought across the ocean as were some wheel-lock guns, but many of the early firearms used in America were matchlocks. There was a major reason for this. Matchlock guns were much cheaper than wheel-locks because they were easier to make, and cost was a big factor with most of the

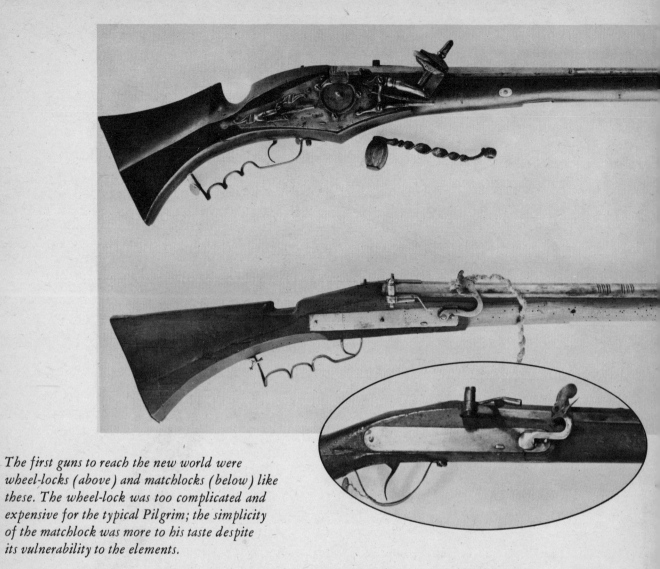

The first guns to reach the new world were wheel-locks (above) and matchlocks (below) like these. The wheel-lock was too complicated and expensive for the typical Pilgrim; the simplicity of the matchlock was more to his taste despite its vulnerability to the elements.

colonists, with their limited resources.

The wheel-lock mechanism is somewhat complicated. A spanner or key, like that used in winding a clock, was employed to wind a spring-controlled serrated wheel. When the wheel was released by the trigger it was spun against a chunk of pyrite or flint clamped in a hinged arm pulled down to make contact with the wheel. This created the sparks which ignited a small powder charge whose flash in turn ignited the main barrel charge. The matchlock was much simpler. A hemp cord, treated to make it burn slowly, was held in a movable serpentine arm. This cord was

called the *match*. When action was expected, it was lighted. The glowing end could then be lowered into the flash pan by action of a simple trigger device and—*boom!*—the charge roared out of the barrel, belching fire and smoke. In passing it should be noted that wheel-lock guns, while used very little in America, were the subjects of some of the finest decorative art work in the 16th and 17th centuries as the prized possessions of European noblemen.

As the colonial conditions and needs became better known, it was found that, other than for its capacity of instilling fear in the

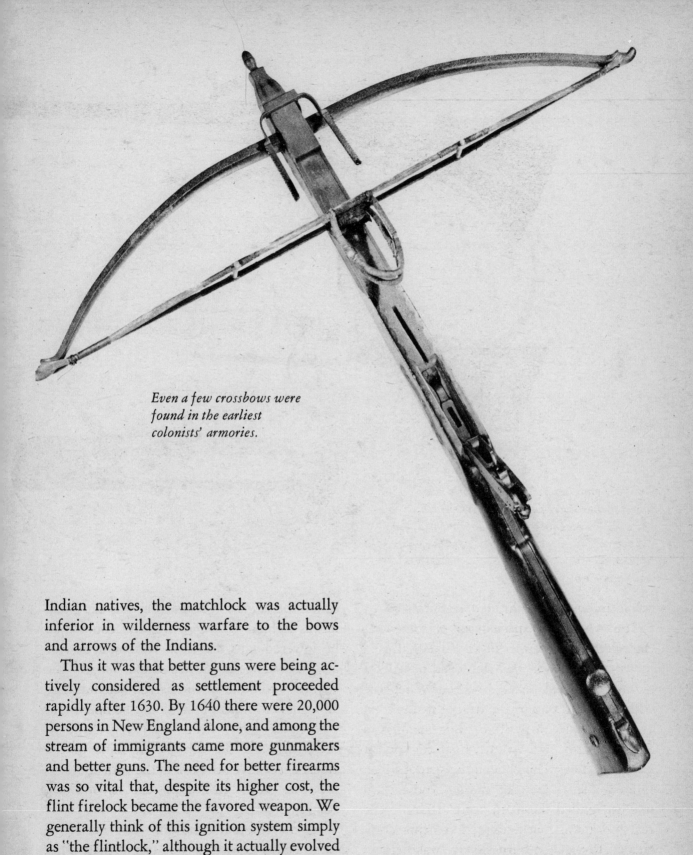

Even a few crossbows were found in the earliest colonists' armories.

Indian natives, the matchlock was actually inferior in wilderness warfare to the bows and arrows of the Indians.

Thus it was that better guns were being actively considered as settlement proceeded rapidly after 1630. By 1640 there were 20,000 persons in New England alone, and among the stream of immigrants came more gunmakers and better guns. The need for better firearms was so vital that, despite its higher cost, the flint firelock became the favored weapon. We generally think of this ignition system simply as "the flintlock," although it actually evolved in five or six steps—from the snaphaunce, in

Though a wheel-lock found in the colonies would be a plain, unornamented arm, some 17th century European noblemen considered arms art objects as well as weapons, as seen in this example.

*Two examples of an early
form of flintlock called the
"dog lock." Note the external
sear located behind the
hammer.*

which the striking face is forged separately from the steel or flash-pan cover, down through the dog lock, miquelet, Scandinavian snap lock, and on to the improved English and French locks with safety and damp-proof features. Whatever the variation, all used the flint and steel principle.

While the early smoothbore shoulder arms were known by such names as *arquebus, caliver* and *musket,* it was the term musket which came to prevail in the flintlock period. This period continued from the 1600s well into the 1800s, the most extended period for any one form of firearms ignition in America. ✥

CHAPTER TWO
The Colonial Expansion

While the English colonists were busy establishing their foothold along the New England coast, the Dutch moved into New York and up the Hudson River establishing "New Netherland." Having had little success along the southern coasts, the French had turned northward and established themselves in the great St. Lawrence valley.

The Dutch were satisfied to limit themselves to the islands at the mouth of the Hudson River along with the lands up and inland from the Hudson and along the Delaware, Swedes in this latter area giving way to the Dutch. The French, however, were more ambitious and the journeys of Champlain, Marquette, Joliet and La Salle provided enthusiastic new assessments of the continent's potential. These ambitious explorations also laid the foundation for bitter conflicts.

White settlers at first had a precarious foothold in the midst of a native population of savage Indian tribes. Starting with the Pequot War in 1637, Indian conflicts forced the colonists to keep their powder dry and their guns close at hand. There followed in quick succession wars between the English and French, with Indian partisan allies on both sides. From 1689 until 1763 what are generally bunched together as the French and Indian wars flared intermittently in various degrees of violence. It took courage to migrate to America in those years.

The colonists were caught in the middle of this struggle of old rivals for supremacy on the American continent. France and England committed large numbers of their regular army troops to the battles. In the end, England triumphed and France was forced to give up her American colonies. The area under Dutch control was also lost to the British, and the town of New Amsterdam became New York.

All this militant action involved many guns;

Among the earliest military arms found in the colonies were French muskets like this example from the Charleville Armory.

the colonial gunsmiths increased in number and were kept very busy. The major weapons of the regular troops sent to America by France were primarily flintlock full-stock muskets. The French were the first to establish uniformity in their military weapons, and by 1717 their issue arms, made in the French armories at Charleville, Maubeuge and St. Etienne, were as uniform as possible for the manufacturing capabilities of the times. Thus we can identify French muskets by model years such as 1717, 1728, 1746, 1754, 1763, 1777, etc.

British military arms were similar to those of the French except for generally bulkier stocks. Their barrels were held to the stock by transverse pins that went through the forestock wood and through lugs welded to the underside of the barrels, whereas the barrels of French guns were usually secured to the stock by encircling iron bands. British military arms were usually stamped with the ruling monarch's cypher, and often bore the word TOWER along with a broad arrow symbol, the sign of government ownership. The British musket was affectionately known as the "Brown Bess" after its browned steel finish and Queen Elizabeth I, who reigned from 1558 to 1603.

The ubiquitous Brown Bess was the arm of the British soldier.

Practically all flintlock muskets of the pre-Revolutionary period had in common a one-piece full stock, one in which the forepart extended under the barrel almost to the muzzle, a smoothbore barrel usually of 75 caliber or more, and a lock mechanism coupled to a trigger. The trigger released the spring-tensioned cock (hammer) which struck a frizzen (or steel), an extension of the pan cover with a flint held in its jaws, causing sparks that ignited the pan powder—a flash in the pan—and igniting the main barrel charge through a small vent or opening leading into the bore. Minor differences in the shape of the stock and the fittings such as trigger guard, buttplate (if any), fore-ends, ferrules or inlays were common. Brass and iron were the metals used.

One of the first students of colonial period arms to preserve his findings for us in books was Charles Winthrop Sawyer of Boston. Mr. Sawyer's first book, *Firearms in American History,* was published in 1910 and deals primarily with long arms of the period 1600-1800. This was followed by a book devoted to the revolver in 1911, a book titled *United States Single Shot Martial Pistols* in 1913, and in 1920 a fourth book titled *Our Rifles* featur-

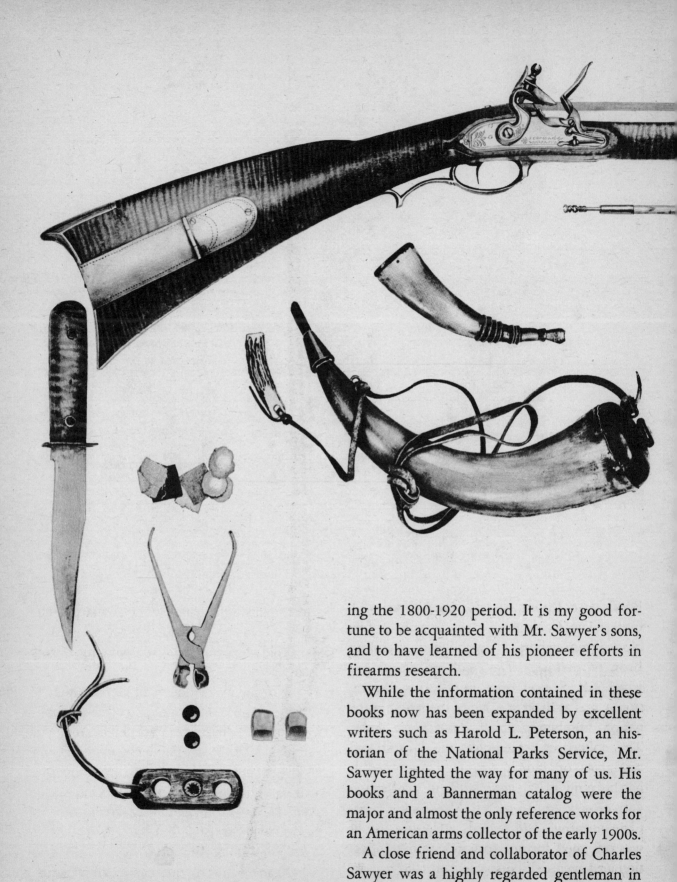

ing the 1800-1920 period. It is my good fortune to be acquainted with Mr. Sawyer's sons, and to have learned of his pioneer efforts in firearms research.

While the information contained in these books now has been expanded by excellent writers such as Harold L. Peterson, an historian of the National Parks Service, Mr. Sawyer lighted the way for many of us. His books and a Bannerman catalog were the major and almost the only reference works for an American arms collector of the early 1900s.

A close friend and collaborator of Charles Sawyer was a highly regarded gentleman in

(Facing page) A fine example of a true Kentucky (Pennsylvania) rifle of the post-revolutionary War period (about 1800) with a complete set of contemporary accoutrements. Its present day owner, Joel Gross of Los Angeles, has bagged several deer with it.

America's bicentennial has spurred a growing interest in our firearms heritage. As the supply of original antique arms dwindles, a number of modern gunmakers has turned to the manufacture of replicas. A close copy of the French Model 1763 Charleville musket, this newly made muzzle-loader would serve as a fireplace decorator or on the firing line at a modern day turkey shoot.

Providence, Rhode Island, named Charles D. Cook. The Cook mansion was only a few blocks from where I lived when attending Brown University. The Cook collection (on which Mr. Sawyer drew heavily for illustrations) was at that time one of the finest in the nation, numbering about 1500 choice items. The collection represented the largest and best group of colonial arms ever assembled. It has been my privilege to study this collection very closely and to review Mr. Cook's glass-plate negatives and records at leisure, for it was my good fortune to purchase the collection and eventually disperse it in 1952.

CHAPTER THREE
Early Native American Guns

he identification of colonial arms is often a difficult task. There are certain native characteristics on some, however, that provide assurance that the gun was stocked and assembled by a colonial gunmaker. Locks and barrels were frequently imported and marked with the name of a London or Birmingham gunsmith, but a good key is provided by the design of the stock.

The most distinctive stocks on colonial arms are popularly called "club" stocks. Club stocks often have no buttplate; the butt has practically no curve where it rests against the shoulder and there are short slanting grooves immediately back of the wrist. Colonial guns of this period are often marked only by the maker's initials and the gunsmiths who made them are practically impossible to identify. Barrel lengths had a wide range from 40″ to 72″. Bores were seldom under 80 caliber. The locks could have a simple flintlock mechanism, or be of the early dog lock pattern with its catch or cog that fitted into a notch at the rear of the cock and served as a safety. The illustrations of these heavy muskets will describe them better than my words.

It is claimed by some that the colonial club stock muskets were made nowhere else than in New England. This may be true, or a few may have been copied and turned out by the Dutch gunmakers along the Hudson. These Dutch gunmakers, however, developed a distinctive flintlock model of their own. This has come to be called the "Hudson River fowler." These guns had an extremely long barrel and it is believed their major use was in harvesting waterfowl along the river and the many small lakes of the region.

For upland shooting, lighter guns with shorter barrels eventually came from the workbenches of the early gunsmiths. Some had no buttplates, all had the gooseneck form of cock

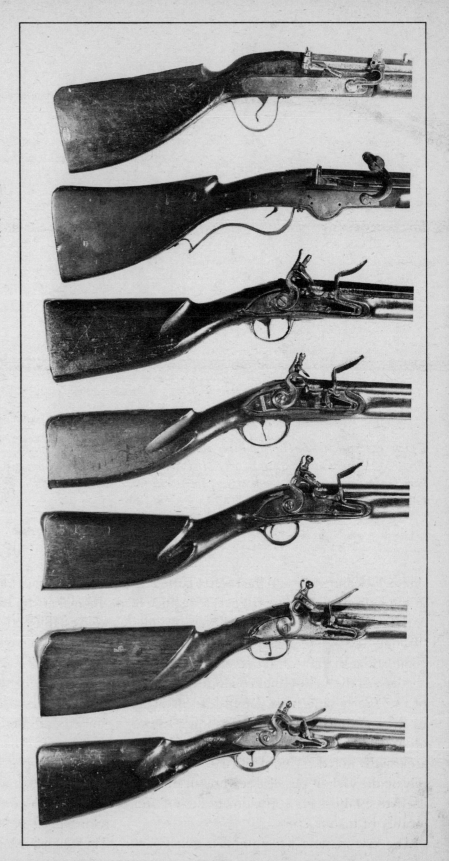

Colonial long guns from matchlocks (above) through flintlocks. Note the club-like stock shape, characteristic of the earliest examples.

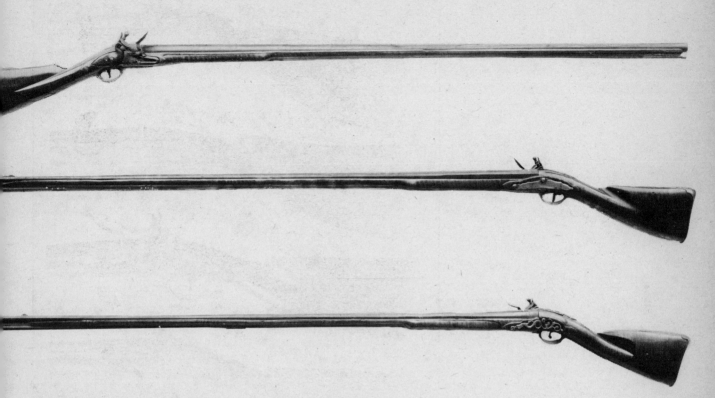

Dutch settlers along the Hudson River developed their own distinct style of flintlock. Known to collectors as the "Hudson River fowler," these long-barrel arms saw duty both as military weapons and game getters. From the Glode M. Requa collection.

on the lock and some had the reverse curled tip at the bottom end of the trigger, a distinctive early feature. Their buttstocks were thinner through and lighter, with a more prominent comb and a sharper drop than before.

Many of the names found on locks or barrels of these early guns have defied identification by those authors of books containing a listing of American gunmakers. If listed at all, they are usually noted as "unidentified." One must rely on the various physical features of the gun itself to establish its approximate period and locality of manufacture.

The raw materials from which guns were made became locally available to the colonial gunmakers by the mid 1600s. An iron works was established near Lynn, Massachusetts in 1643, and the wood for stocks was abundant. Powder mills were soon in operation at Andover, Stoughton, Dorchester and other places. It was reported in 1676 that "In Massachusetts all mechanical arts and occupations thrive well. The colonists make iron as good as the Spanish, cast their own cannon, and manufacture powder as good and strong as the best English powder." Similar advances were taking place in New York and Pennsylvania. Thus it may be seen that the necessary steps

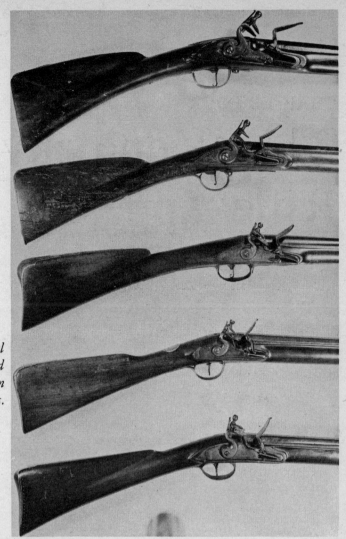

These later-style colonial flintlocks are lighter and more graceful than their predecessors.

were being taken in the colonies to let them become self-reliant.

There was not much in the way of change or novelty in the design of muskets through the late 1600s or in the 1700s up to about 1775. The major progress had been made in improving manufacturing methods, the development of water power to run gunmaking machinery, an increase in iron and powder production and an increase in the number of skilled craftsmen working in the gun trade. During this period there had been but little attention to the making of pistols in America, although officers of the French and English military forces usually carried them.

CHAPTER FOUR
The "Kentucky" Rifle Appears

A major step in American gunmaking had been taking place down in Pennsylvania, where the ports of Philadelphia and Baltimore had begun to rival Boston and New York. From these debarkation points many emigrants moved inland, although a few settled in or near Philadelphia. The majority were of German or Swiss lineage. Thus it was that throughout Pennsylvania, and to a lesser extent in Maryland, Virginia and the Carolinas, there were among these seekers of a better life in America many talented gunmakers. The armsmaker's trade was very active and respected in Europe. The new colonies

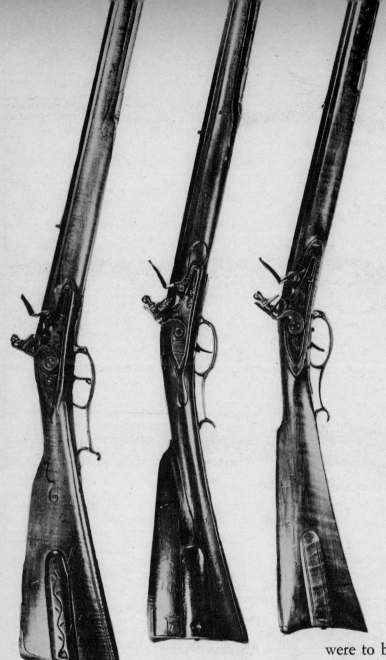

The Pennsylvania rifle, better known as the Kentucky rifle, is descended from the European hunting rifle called the Jaeger.

were to benefit greatly by this exodus from "the Old Country."

A great majority of the guns made in New England, New York, and in most of the populated areas close to the eastern seaboard were smoothbore muskets. It was different, however, in backwoods Pennsylvania and other nearby areas including Kentucky and Tennessee.

We must retrace our steps a bit to better understand what had been going on in these areas after the Germans, Swiss and some French Huguenots had fanned out to places like Lancaster, York, Hagerstown and up the

Note the points of resemblance between the Kentucky rifles and the Jaegers in this group.

Susquehanna and Schuylkill rivers in Pennsylvania. Many of these places had good locations for water mills, ideal for power in running gunmaking machinery.

Here were cradled the long rifles we have come to call "Kentuckys." A rifle, of course, indicates a gun with a grooved bore. The principle of rifling is many years old, having been used in central Europe during the early wheel-lock period. Its use then, however, was limited to hunting arms of the wealthier land-owners. The wheel-lock had not been considered seriously by European nations as a military arm because of its weight, compli-

cated mechanism, slow loading process, and high cost.

The idea of rifling persisted, however, and in the Germanic countries advances in grooved barrels were made as ignition systems proceeded into the flintlock period. For hunting in the German forests a short, thick-stocked rifle known as a Jäger (or Jaeger) gained popularity, and some were issued to special German military units. When the Hessian mercenaries were sent to America to fight for the British during the Revolution, many carried rifles of this kind. It was perhaps just retribution that those German mercenaries

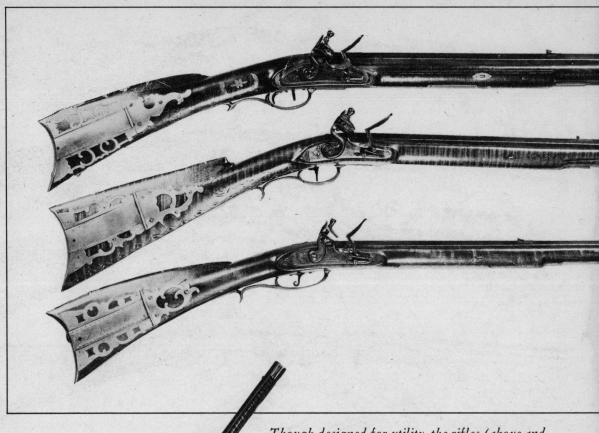

Though designed for utility, the rifles (above and on facing page) from many frontier makers boasted fancy patchboxes and elaborately carved stocks. From the Charles D. Cook collection.

One of the most distinctive features of the Pennsylvania or Kentucky rifle is its graceful beauty.

should in some cases face embattled patriots armed with better rifles than their own, produced by German-Americans!

Muskets had been produced in the colonies for a long time when Martin Meylin, credited as one of the progenitors of the Pennsylvania or "Kentucky" long rifles, opened his shop in 1719. Other gunsmiths soon followed his lead in reshaping the German Jaeger into a gun more suited to the American needs. Barrels were made longer, bores smaller, stocks lighter, and fittings were of easy-to-work brass. The native hard maple replaced walnut for stocks. Ramrods were of hickory rather

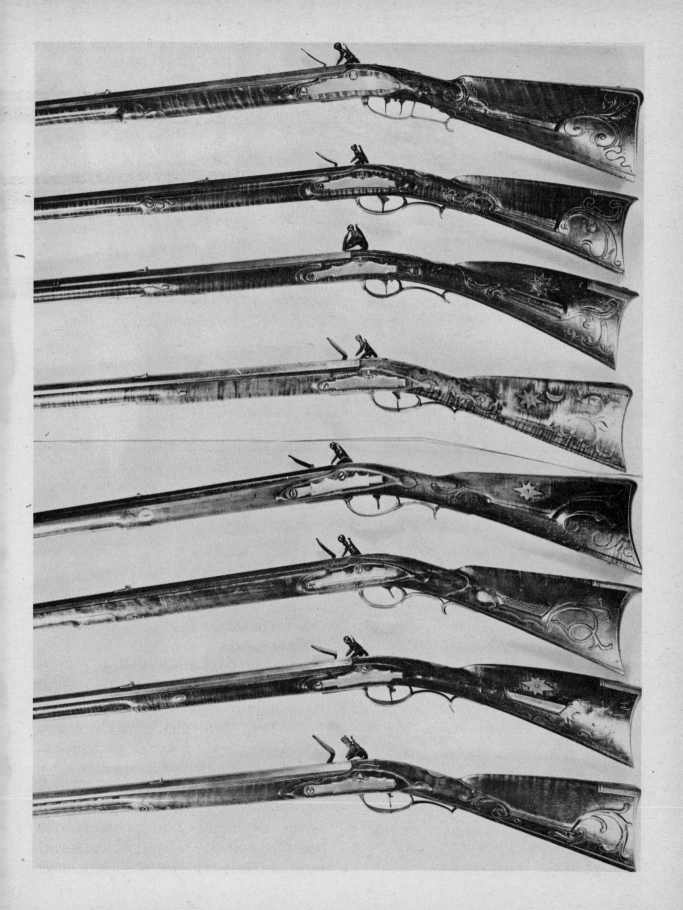

Much rarer than Kentucky rifles, Kentucky pistols such as these matched pairs are a collector's prize. From the Herman P. Dean collection.

than steel (which tended to deform the ball), and the ball itself was made tight in the bore yet seated easily by means of a greased patch of cloth or thin deerskin. All these changes had a practical reason, and the improvements were so great that the long rifles became the first unique American firearm.

As the population increased, forests were cleared, towns appeared, and the frontiers were expanded. In all this progress, the rifle was as important a tool as the axe and the plow. Designed as an arm for the hunter, it provided much of his meat needs along with skins for clothing and other by-products. It provided the means from which some derived their livelihood and was the major instrument of personal and community security. While not designed as a military weapon, the long rifle rendered valuable service in the hands of special military rifle units.

When General Braddock's Coldstream Guards faced annihilation on the Monongahela by a French and Indian force in 1775, it was a small group of colonial riflemen commanded by a young aide named George Washington who, employing the same battle tactics as the Indians, saved the rout of the Englishmen from becoming a complete massacre.

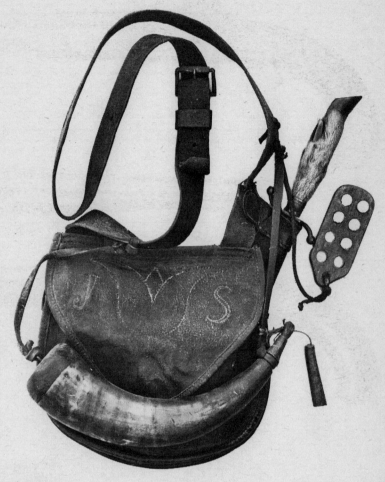

His accessory bag and powder horn were indispensable to the early rifleman. The bag carried bullets, bullet mould, patches, powder measure and spare flints, while the horn was an easy-to-use waterproof dispenser for powder.

Mr. Sawyer tells us that colonial riflemen contributed greatly to the capture of Quebec in 1759 by mowing down advancing ranks of French veterans with deadly accurate rifle fire. The French forces were commanded by General Montcalm, who was killed in that action. Major General James Wolfe, on the English side, had ten battalions of infantry, six companies of rangers, artillery, engineers and a Grenadier corps in his command. There were other occasions, too, when colonial militiamen performed valiantly in the British cause, although some friction was developing between Colonials and British regulars.

CHAPTER FIVE
Beginnings of the Revolution

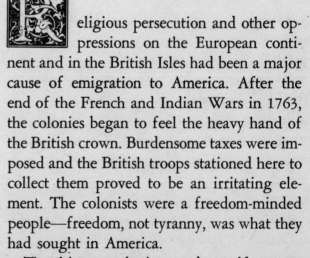

Religious persecution and other oppressions on the European continent and in the British Isles had been a major cause of emigration to America. After the end of the French and Indian Wars in 1763, the colonies began to feel the heavy hand of the British crown. Burdensome taxes were imposed and the British troops stationed here to collect them proved to be an irritating element. The colonists were a freedom-minded people—freedom, not tyranny, was what they had sought in America.

The thirteen colonies, used to self-government, strongly resented "taxation without representation" and trial without jury by admiralty courts. Incensed by British arrogance, nine colonies adopted a "Declaration of Rights." In the Virginia House of Burgesses Patrick Henry warned King George III of possible dire consequences by stating, "If this be treason, make the most of it." He is also remembered for his impassioned plea of "Give me liberty or give me death." Patrick Henry reflected a widely held sentiment, for on July 4, 1776, after violence in Boston and gunfire at Lexington, Concord and Bunker Hill, representatives of the American colonies, assembled in Philadelphia, signed a "Declaration of In-

dependence." The war was on and the colonists looked to their guns.

Among the first acts of the united American colonies, henceforth known as the United States, was formation of "Committees of Safety." These committees vigorously set out to encourage armsmakers to become involved in the manufacturing or repairing of arms suitable for militia use. The role of gunmakers was so vital to the country's needs that the Continental Congress asked that they be exempted from military service.

In New England emphasis was given to producing smoothbore muskets, while down

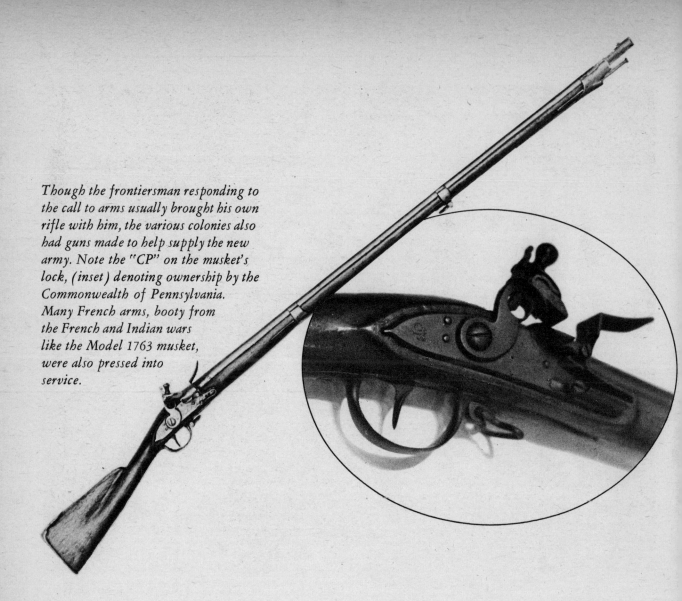

Though the frontiersman responding to the call to arms usually brought his own rifle with him, the various colonies also had guns made to help supply the new army. Note the "CP" on the musket's lock, (inset) denoting ownership by the Commonwealth of Pennsylvania. Many French arms, booty from the French and Indian wars like the Model 1763 musket, were also pressed into service.

in Pennsylvania it is said that orders for 1000 plain rifled guns were placed. In quick order twelve rifle companies were formed, eight from Pennsylvania, two from Maryland, and two from Virginia. Jacob Ferree, a gunsmith and powder manufacturer, was given charge of the French Creek Powder Mill at Kimberton, Pennsylvania, while expanded efforts were made not only to obtain guns and powder but also lead and flints to meet the needs of war.

It was a member of one of these new rifle companies, Timothy Murphy, who, on a brisk October day of 1777, lined his sights on the

resplendent uniform of General Simon Fraser, a very capable officer of the British Army. The powder charge in Murphy's rifle responded sharply to the sparks of flint striking steel and a lethal lead ball sped unerringly to its target.

The loss of General Fraser was a factor in General Burgoyne's surrender to the Americans at Saratoga soon thereafter. While it must be noted that the long rifles were used sparingly and only by special units, their use often was crucial to American successes.

Another such occasion was at King's Mountain, North Carolina, on October 7, 1780, when a force of 900 Americans led by "Noli-

Major Patrick Ferguson, whose breech-loading rifle might have changed the course of history if it had been adopted, loses his life to a Yankee marksman at the Battle of King's Mountain.

chucky Jack" Sevier, William Campbell and Benjamin Cleveland soundly defeated a large British force there led by Major Patrick Ferguson. In this battle the backwoods Americans armed with long rifles killed and wounded 242 British and loyalist militiamen and took 664 prisoners. This victory broke the back of British power in the South. Major Ferguson, the brave British commander, was killed.

It was ironic that this brilliant young Englishman, only 36 years old, should be killed by a rifle ball. He had but a few years before convinced the British Board of Ordnance to have 100 breech-loading flintlock rifles of his

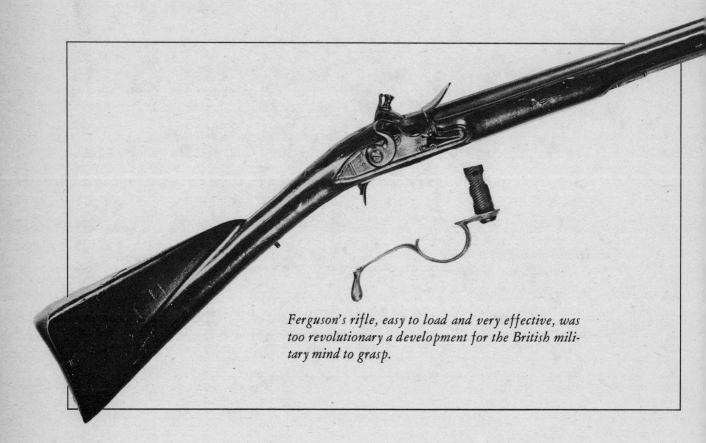

Ferguson's rifle, easy to load and very effective, was too revolutionary a development for the British military mind to grasp.

design made up by William Grice, Benjamin Willets, Mathias Barker and Galton & Son. A few others were made by John Hunt, Durs Egg and perhaps others.

One hundred recruits, mainly from the 6th and 14th Regiments, were issued the fine new Ferguson flintlock breechloaders and sent to America, where they arrived on May 24, 1777.

This rifle group under Major Ferguson was active in the Battle of Brandywine Hill and several other engagements, in one of which Ferguson had received a severe wound in the arm. In view of Ferguson's temporary incapacity, General Howe decided to disband Fer-

guson's rifle company, Howe's views being those of many military men of the time that it was musket volleys and bayonet charges that really won battles. When Ferguson had recovered and was given command of a battalion for action in the South, it is unlikely that even one of his rifles was in that force. That was perhaps fortunate for the Americans as Ferguson had demonstrated at Woolwich, England, that his guns were capable of shooting five or six times a minute, were very resistant to damp, could place a bullet regularly in a small bullseye target 100 yards distant, and had given good accuracy at 400 yards. This

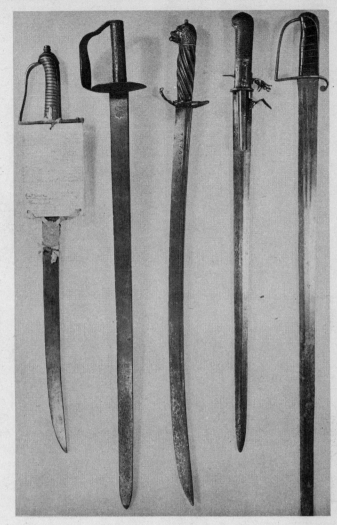

Swords were also important weapons of the colonial period. Second from right in this group is a sword incorporating a flintlock pistol, while the sword at the left belonged to naval hero John Barry who was the first U.S. Commodore.

performance far exceeded anything the Brown Bess or even the average American "Kentucky" rifle could provide.

After the War for Independence was settled for all practical purposes by Cornwallis' surrender at Yorktown on October 19, 1781, final treaties were ratified by the United States Congress on January 14, 1784. It was then hoped that peace would come to the land at last.

CHAPTER SIX

The New Nation
Faces Peace

he colonies had paid a costly price for freedom. Among the many casualties four members of my own family gave their lives in the struggle. But now the new nation, fortunate in the guidance of such men as Washington, Franklin, Jefferson and others faced its new responsibilities with vigor and courage.

There were approximately 4,000,000 Americans in the 13 states by 1790, with Pennsylvania, Massachusetts and New York (in that order), having the greatest populations. In ten years another 1,000,000 would have spread over the land.

With the recent war's urgent need for arms still fresh in mind, military leaders of the new nation began to set up plans to insure adequate military supplies in the event of future emergencies. By this time areas of industrial activity had formed in New England, especially along the Connecticut River. In the cities of Boston, New York and Philadelphia many small shops had grown into factories. Lancaster, Pennsylvania, had become a center of trade and manufacturing, the Leman gunmaking factory there being especially prominent.

During the time of the Revolution, American gunmaking plants had operated at full capacity, for in 1774 Great Britain had cut off all shipments of arms to the colonies. Those proprietors whose shops had expanded to the status of a manufactory were expected to have three or four barrel forges, a grinding mill, a lock shop with six or seven forges, benches for several dozen filers and as many for gunstock makers. There should be a brass foundry for mountings that included several finishing benches, a couple of forges for bayonets and metal ramrods together with a mill for grinding and polishing them, and finally an assembly room.

It was to these well-established gunmakers

GENERAL VIEW.

*An early view of Springfield
Armory taken from an
old print.*

that the government now looked for its arms. However, a government-owned source of supply was also considered desirable and Congress authorized the President to establish one or more places for the manufacturing of U.S. arms. As a result, Springfield Armory (Massachusetts) started its long and illustrious career in 1795 and Harper's Ferry Armory (West Virginia) in 1796. In 1797 the Virginia Manufactory at Richmond was established and continued to make and repair weapons up to the 1860s.

CHAPTER SEVEN

The U.S. Musket Model 1795

The first pattern of U.S. shoulder arm to be approved by the Ordnance Department followed the design of the French Model 1763 musket. France, by its great aid in supplying arms and its vital naval and land force assistance during the war, was in great favor after the hostilities. The Marquis de Lafayette had become an American hero. Not only was the pattern of France's shoulder arms favored, but the first U.S. martial pistols were built on the French 1777 pistol design.

Production of muskets was at first slow in the national armories. The initial model, known as the U.S. Model 1795, was not being produced at the armories in sufficient quantities to meet needs so Congress authorized the purchase of 40,000 stands of arms from private armsmakers. These first contractors of government arms are believed to have been Eli Whitney, D. Gilbert, E. Brown, E. Buell and J. McCormick.

Of these contractors Eli Whitney was to be the most important contributor, introducing a system of interchangeable parts formed from stampings and finished to uniform dimensions by sets of gauges. Other contractors to whom the government turned for later arms were Simeon North of Berlin and Middletown, Connecticut, Asa Waters of Sutton (now Millbury), Massachusetts, Lemuel Pomeroy of Pittsfield, Massachusetts, Nathan Starr and the Johnsons of Middletown, Connecticut, Stephen Jenks of Providence, Rhode Island, and Henry Deringer of Philadelphia, Pennsylvania.

Simeon North was selected to be the first official U.S. pistol maker and, in partnership with his brother-in-law Elisha Cheney, produced 500 pistols of the French 1777 pattern which are now collectors' items that are very rare and valuable.

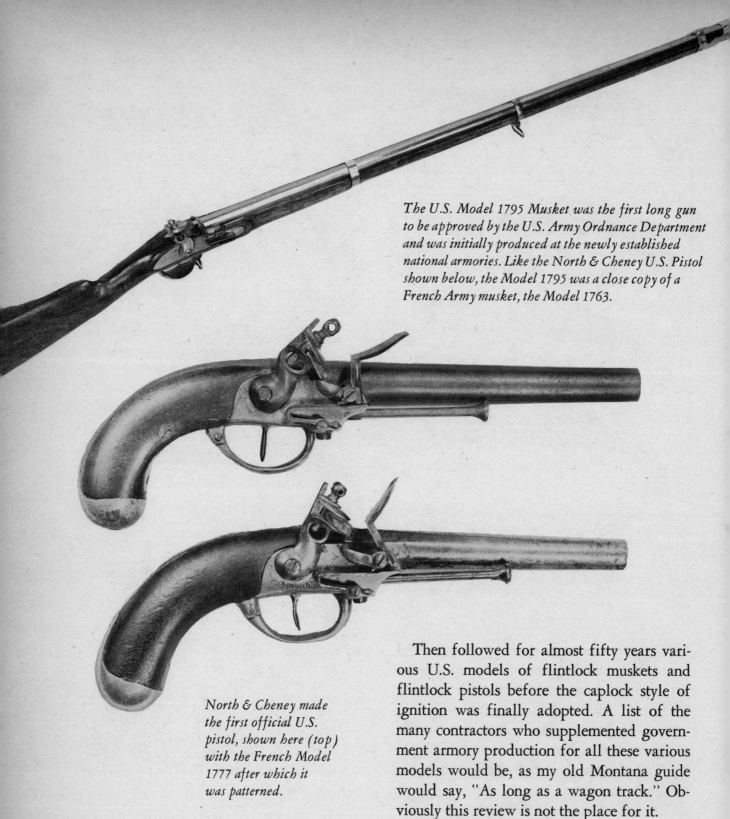

The U.S. Model 1795 Musket was the first long gun to be approved by the U.S. Army Ordnance Department and was initially produced at the newly established national armories. Like the North & Cheney U.S. Pistol shown below, the Model 1795 was a close copy of a French Army musket, the Model 1763.

North & Cheney made the first official U.S. pistol, shown here (top) with the French Model 1777 after which it was patterned.

Then followed for almost fifty years various U.S. models of flintlock muskets and flintlock pistols before the caplock style of ignition was finally adopted. A list of the many contractors who supplemented government armory production for all these various models would be, as my old Montana guide would say, "As long as a wagon track." Obviously this review is not the place for it.

All the activity in obtaining arms for the state militias and regular armed forces had good justification. Many European nations and some of our American neighbors were jealous of this fledgling country with its

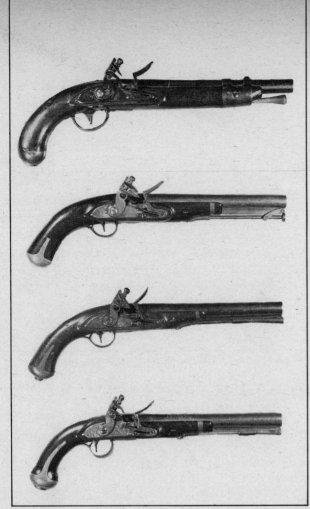

A variety of U.S. martial flint pistols followed the North & Cheney. Shown here (from top) are: Springfield Model 1818, Richmond Manufactory (1813), another Richmond Manufactory dated 1812, and a Harper's Ferry dated 1808.

boundless resources and great potentials. Our love affair with France cooled quickly when French raids were made on U.S. shipping in 1798, but better relations were restored in 1803 when France's claims to a great section of the central continent were transferred to the United States by what is known as "The Louisiana Purchase."

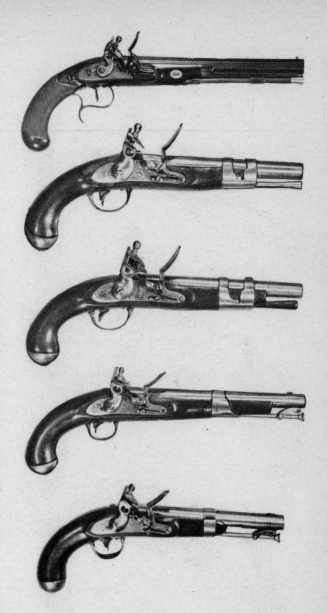

Simeon North was the most prolific flintlock pistol maker for the U.S. government. At the top of the group is one of his graceful duelers for the civilian market for comparison, followed by the Military Models 1813, 1816 and 1819. At the bottom is a Johnson Model 1836.

CHAPTER EIGHT

The War of 1812

till smarting 30 years after its defeat in the American war for independence, Britain began to seize American ships and furnish arms to the American Indians who raided our western borders. These acts could not be tolerated so Congress voted a Declaration of War against England in 1812, proceeded to increase the army from 11,744 to 44,500 and called out the militia. The U.S. Navy had grown to a force to be reckoned with during the post-Revolution years and our merchant ships were enjoying a very profitable international trade. Naval and marine forces have always drawn heavily on the productivity of gunmakers and the War of 1812 was no exception.

Land action in the first years of the war brought few successes to U.S. militiamen or to the few regulars. In August a British force of 4,000 landed near Washington, defeated the Americans at Bladensburg, and burned the Capitol and the White House.

A much different situation prevailed at sea, however, where among the victories recorded was that of the U.S.S. *Constitution* (Old Ironsides) over the *Guerriere*. Using Captain James Lawrence's dying words, "Don't give up the ship," as a slogan, Admiral Perry's

flotilla defeated a British fleet on Lake Erie. Other naval victories followed.

The final chapter of the War of 1812 was fought east of New Orleans on January 8, 1815. A force of 5300 veterans led by Major General Edward Pakenham, having been put ashore from British warships, advanced on a lesser assorted force led by General Andrew Jackson, a border pioneer from Tennessee. There followed the most amazing one-sided battle recorded in the annals of American warfare. When the smoke had cleared the red coats of 2000 British soldiers, including General Pakenham himself, were stained with the

An "India Pattern" Brown Bess, the musket carried by British "Beefeaters" during the War of 1812.

darker crimson of death. American casualties were unbelievably small. General Jackson reported of his force six killed and seven wounded!

There is an old Latin quotation which, in translation, reads: "Whom God wills to destroy, He first makes mad." Certainly it was sheer madness for the British to advance in close formation across an open field against an entrenched force which included keen-eyed backwoods riflemen from Tennessee and Kentucky. The British called these men "the dirty-shirts"; a better name would have been "the sharpshooters."

Twelve hundred British Brown Bess muskets were left on the field that day. They had scarcely gotten in firing range, so deadly had been the long-range fire of General Jackson's men.

To be objective, one cannot say that the Kentucky long rifles deserve all the credit for the victory. It was eventually the deciding factor, but not the entire story. An earlier clash with the enemy on the night of December 23 had involved hand-to-hand fighting with swords, belt axes and bayonets. Although inconclusive, this had served a useful purpose, turning British contempt into cau-

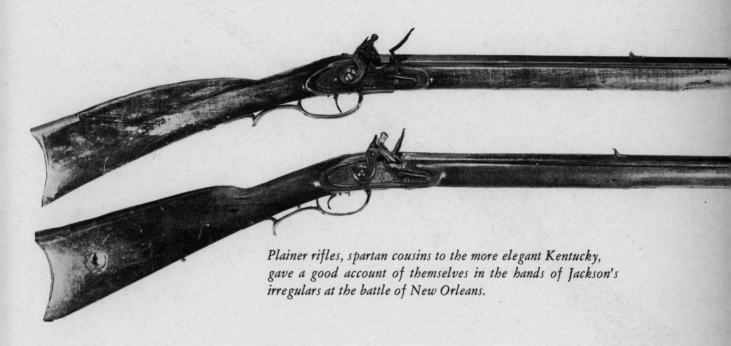

Plainer rifles, spartan cousins to the more elegant Kentucky, gave a good account of themselves in the hands of Jackson's irregulars at the battle of New Orleans.

tion and indecisive delay which gave American forces an opportunity to become firmly entrenched. Fifteen cannon of various types, from brass 6-pounders to a 32-pound monster had been put in place along the breastworks. Muskets of the infantrymen, militiamen and others stood ready to pour a withering fire and mount a bayonet attack against any who might survive the fire of the riflemen or the cannon.

Dependable guns in the hands of courageous American fighting men turned back the British bid to grasp the "beauty and booty" of New Orleans. It has been said that only he

who realizes the intimate relations between the tools of a nation and its institutions really understands its history. The story of American-made guns embraces not only the gun itself but the men who designed, made and used it, along with the economic contributions in communities where it was made. ☙

CHAPTER NINE
America's Armsmakers Expand

 majority of the Kentucky rifles such as those used at New Orleans was made in relatively small shops spread westward from Philadelphia in a fan-shaped pattern, some eventually locating as far west as Pittsburgh. A few gunmakers in Massachusetts such as Silas Allen, Martin Smith and Henry Pratt made full-stock rifles with long, narrow, brass patchboxes having no side bars. These guns had a tendency toward the more severe English architecture, rather than that of the Pennsylvania Deutsche.

Philadelphia and its environs saw great strides in armsmaking after the Revolution.

John McCormick received a contract for the U.S. Model 1795 musket and also made muskets for the State of Virginia. He failed in 1801 and was succeeded by James Haslett, a very competent gunmaker. The McCormick contracts were filled at the Globe Mill erected for William Penn in 1700. Another early Philadelphia gunmaker, Henry Deringer, became well known for his government arms contracts but he was destined to produce the small caplock pocket pistols that became so popular that all small pistols were soon called "derringers" (the double "r" spelling is correct). The William Henry family was active in the gunmaking trade at Lancaster, and then some members of that family moved east to Philadelphia to establish a factory to produce military and Indian arms for the government and hunting arms for the civilian trade. Another prominent gunmaking family, one whose continuous activity in the field exceeded that of all others, was founded by George W. Tryon in 1811. Tryons continued in the arms trade for five generations.

It is said that the dollar value of all arms manufactured at Philadelphia in 1811, when the Tryon business was founded, totalled only $74,250. But that figure rapidly increased

Sporting arms were also an important product of the new nation's armsmakers. This is a cap-lock single barrel hunting rifle made by R.S. Clark of Albany, N.Y.

and, before many years had passed, Tryon's sales alone exceeded Philadelphia's 1811 total.

The Tryons not only had a good local trade, but they made guns for the Republic of Texas and were selected by the U.S. Government to supply a variety of arms, including guns for the Indians. A majority of these Indian guns were of the flintlock pattern and known as "The Northwest Gun." They were smoothbore, full-stock weapons with large trigger guards and a serpentine sideplate. Over 5000 were made by Tryon alone. After 153 years of operations under the Tryon name

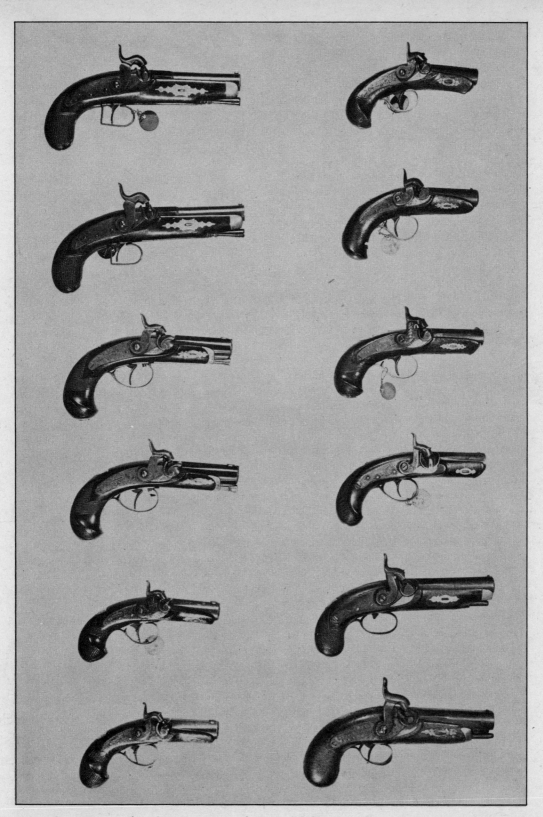

As civilization spread to the west, personal protection became a face-to-face rather than long range proposition. Small pocket pistols, made popular by Henry Deringer of Philadelphia, became widely used.

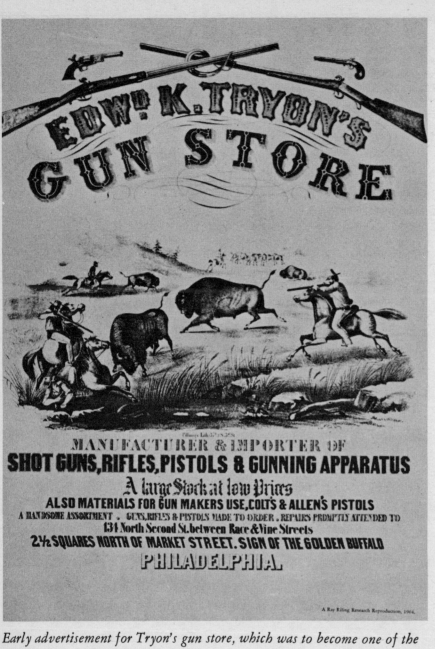

Early advertisement for Tryon's gun store, which was to become one of the nation's longest lived firearms outlets.

Tryon was a leading supplier of guns to the government for the Indian trade, many of which were muskets like this "Northwest Gun."

The U.S. government as well as Indian traders furnished Northwest guns, pipe axes and knives such as these to various Indian tribes. The policy was not without critics along the frontier.

the company lost its identity by merger with a large hardware concern. You might say that the Tryon firm did not die but, like old generals, just faded away.

Some other great names in the gun business at Philadelphia were Kunz, Wurfflein, Evans, Slotter, Constable, Grubb, Butterfield, Bird— the list is long.

CHAPTER TEN

The Guns of the Early West

efore taking a look at further progress in New York and New England, it may be well to let our thoughts travel up the Potomac River to the government armory at Harper's Ferry, West Virginia. It was here that the most graceful single shot flintlock martial pistols (Model 1806) were made along with some equally handsome half-stock flintlock rifles (Models 1803 and 1814). Some of the early model Harper's Ferry rifles are said to have been issued to Lewis and Clark when they made their historic explorations into the Northwest. Of special note is that Harper's Ferry also saw the production of the first U.S. breech-loading flintlock, the Model 1819, which was designed by J.H. Hall. Caplock carbines on this breech-loading principle were later made in Connecticut by S. North and used by the U.S. First Dragoons during the conquest of New Mexico and California.

The interval between the War of 1812 and the Mexican War was a period in which there was a marked progress in industry, agriculture, and an expansion of central government. These years reflect the picture of a hard-working pioneer people reaching out for land, and many faces now turned westward.

But there was time for simple enjoyments, too, such as the shooting matches for a quarter of beef or a turkey at country crossroads. It was also a time for religious activities. For example, the Mormon church was founded in Seneca County, New York, in 1830 by Joseph Smith.

Indian hostilities continued to be a source of trouble for the government and the more adventuresome settlers but finally the Ohio valley, parts of the midwest and the southern regions were made more secure by pushing the Sac and Fox Indians west of the Mississippi; by treaty the Cherokees were moved to

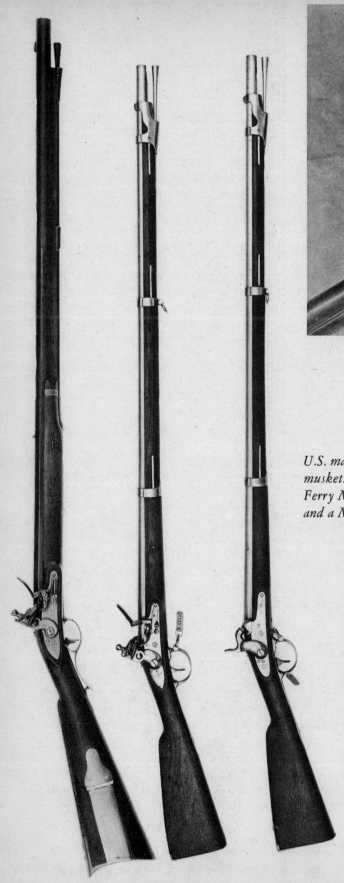

*U.S. martial smoothbore
muskets. From left, the Harper's
Ferry Models 1814 and 1835
and a Model 1842 caplock.*

the "Indian Nations" territory, now Oklahoma.

Settlers who had pushed into the Southwest after the Louisiana Purchase had become restless under very unpopular Mexican rule. Led by Sam Houston, they claimed independence and established the Texas Republic in 1835. This westward movement, which eventually led to the Mexican War, well predated the discovery of gold in California.

Technologically, steam power was being employed in ships and railroads. S.F.B. Morse perfected the telegraph. Great technical strides were being made in many fields such

(Facing page.) Designed by John H. Hall of Yarmouth, Maine, the first U.S. military breechloader was made at Harper's Ferry arsenal as the Model 1819.

A Model 1819 Hall flint-lock breechloader complete with socket bayonet.

as medicine, where an anesthetic was administered for the first time in 1842. The great Erie Canal opened the Mohawk valley to cheap transportation. The nation was on the move.

While the new nation was expanding and great progress was being made in other fields America's gunmakers were not idle. Although it took the U.S. Ordnance Department until 1841 to produce its first caplock rifle (the army stuck to flintlock muskets as late as 1840), the new ignition system had been more quickly accepted by the civilian trade.

In 1807 the Reverend Alexander Forsyth,

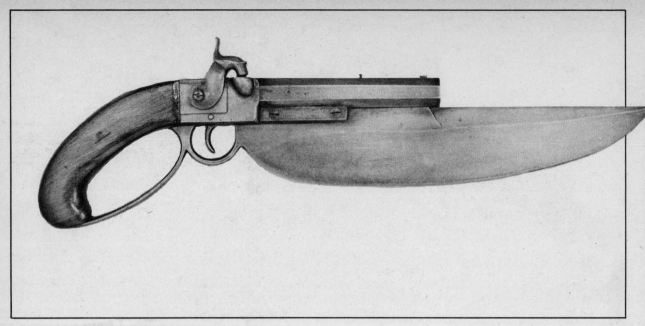

One of the most unusual early U.S. martial arms was the cutlass pistol, made by C. B. Allen under George Elgin's patent.

Principal U.S. single shot caplock pistols were (from top): A. H. Waters, H. Aston & Co. Model 1842, Model 1843 boxlock made by H. Deringer and another Model 1842 by N. P. Ames.

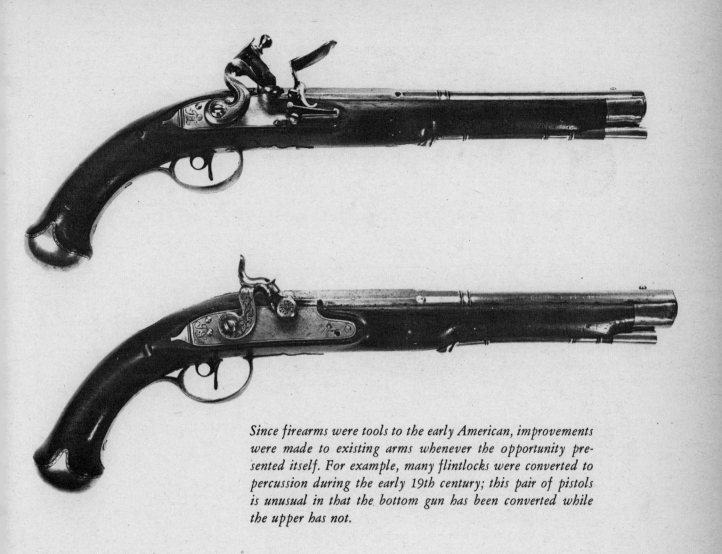

Since firearms were tools to the early American, improvements were made to existing arms whenever the opportunity presented itself. For example, many flintlocks were converted to percussion during the early 19th century; this pair of pistols is unusual in that the bottom gun has been converted while the upper has not.

an amateur chemist of Aberdeenshire, Scotland, had been working with a compound that would detonate when struck sharply. By 1816 an immigrant to America from England named Joshua Shaw put this principle to very practical use by placing the detonating compound in sealed metal cups, which became known as "percussion caps." When a cap was struck sharply by a flat hammer-face the fire passed through the hollow nipple on which it was mounted to fire the powder charge in the barrel.

This system permitted simpler lockwork and was damp proof, thus giving greater assurance against misfires. It had many advantages and but few disadvantages when compared to the flintlock system. It opened up new possibilities for developing practicable multi-shot mechanisms such as repeating arms operated by a revolving cylinder.

Many of the old flintlock guns were converted to the caplock system by installing a new hammer, removing the old battery, and installing a *bolster* or hollow drum into which a percussion nipple could be fitted.

CHAPTER ELEVEN

Sam Colt's Caplock Revolver

amuel Colt was one of the first to see the great possibilities of the new caplock system for repeating arms. He invented what is considered the first successful revolver in 1836, which employed a single barrel combined with a rotating multi-chambered cylinder. Various 5-shot models were made at Paterson, New Jersey, by the Patent Arms Mfg. Co. from 1836 to 1842. Rifles and shotguns using this same revolver principle were also made at the Paterson manufacturing plant.

Ethan Allen of Grafton and Worcester, Massachusetts was another who saw great possibilities in the percussion cap, and in 1837 Allen patented a *multi-barrel* pistol which came to be known as a "pepperbox." Not only were these pepperbox pistols repeating arms, but many of them also employed a relatively new *double-action* firing mechanism; that is, a single pull on the trigger both cocked the hammer and let it drop. Allen's patents were apparently not very protective, for it was not long before other manufacturers in New York and New England were also producing pepperbox pistols. The pepperbox was cheaper to make than the true revolver of the Colt type and thus enjoyed a good sale. It eventu-

ally became popular with miners in the California gold fields.

Following granting of the Colt and Allen patents, there was more inventive activity which in 1837 saw firearms patents issued to Daniel Leavitt, John W. Cochran, and O.W. Whittier. The number of firearms patents issued yearly increased rapidly thereafter until today thousands have been recorded.

From 1836 up to the War between the States was the active period in production of caplock cylinder rifles, with most produced in the 1850s. Not only were bored multichambered cylinders like Colt's used, but

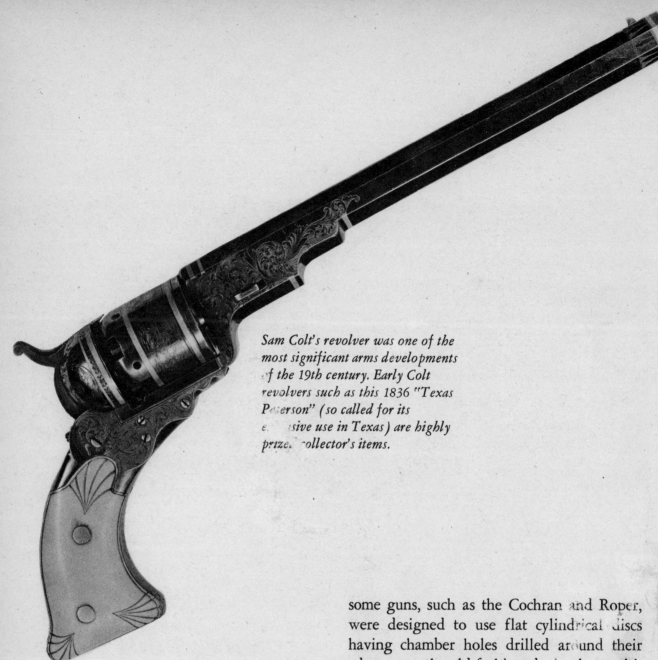

Sam Colt's revolver was one of the most significant arms developments of the 19th century. Early Colt revolvers such as this 1836 "Texas Paterson" (so called for its extensive use in Texas) are highly prized collector's items.

some guns, such as the Cochran and Roper, were designed to use flat cylindrical discs having chamber holes drilled around their edges as on the old-fashioned, circular, multi-hole mouse traps. These were called *turret guns.*

O.W. Whittier and Nichols & Childs followed the lead of Colt's Paterson models. An improved Colt sidehammer model based on Root's patents was introduced in 1855, and for competition the Colt Root model had cylinder rifles made by North & Savage, Allen & Wheelock, Hall, Warner, Roper, Remington and others. Pill-lock (percussion pellets)

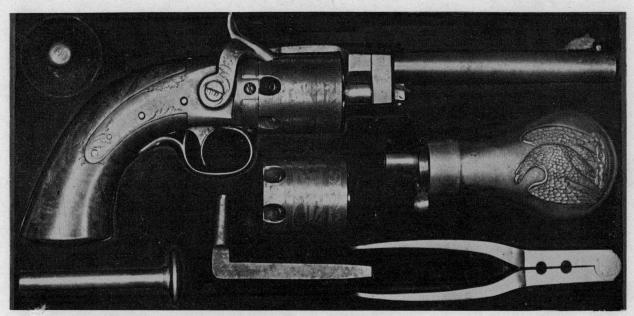

Colt's greatest competitor in the early caplock era was the Massachusetts Arms Co. of Chicopee Falls, Massachusetts. One of their early models, based on the Wesson & Leavitt patent, is shown here cased with accessories. Patent rights were hotly contested between the Massachusetts Arms Co. and Colt.

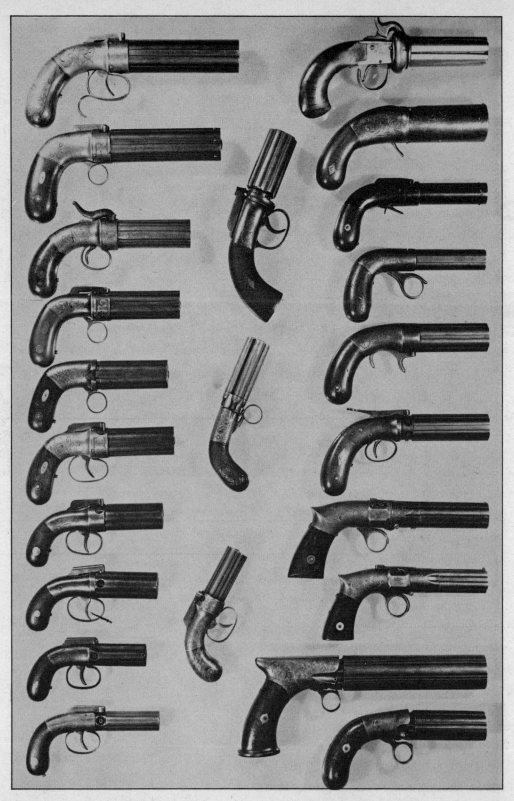

Principal rivals to Colt's patented design were various manufacturers' "pepperboxes." The guns in the left hand column of this group were made by Allen and the others by other makers.

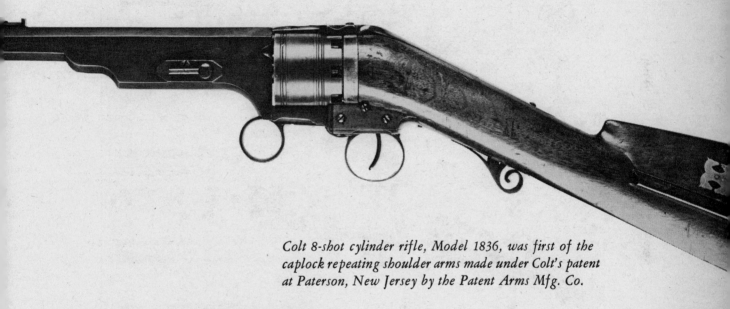

Colt 8-shot cylinder rifle, Model 1836, was first of the caplock repeating shoulder arms made under Colt's patent at Paterson, New Jersey by the Patent Arms Mfg. Co.

cylinder rifles were made by Miller, Brown, Cherington, Volpius, Ormsby, Smith, Bigelow and Billinghurst.

While various experiments in multi-shot firearms had been undertaken during the flintlock period and even earlier, about the only early multi-shot gun that might be called truly successful was the double barrel (side-by-side) flintlock shotgun, with right and left locks. In England, where the best arms were then made, these guns were called birding or fowling pieces. Henry Nock and the Manton brothers—Joseph and John—of London were among the most skilled makers. A

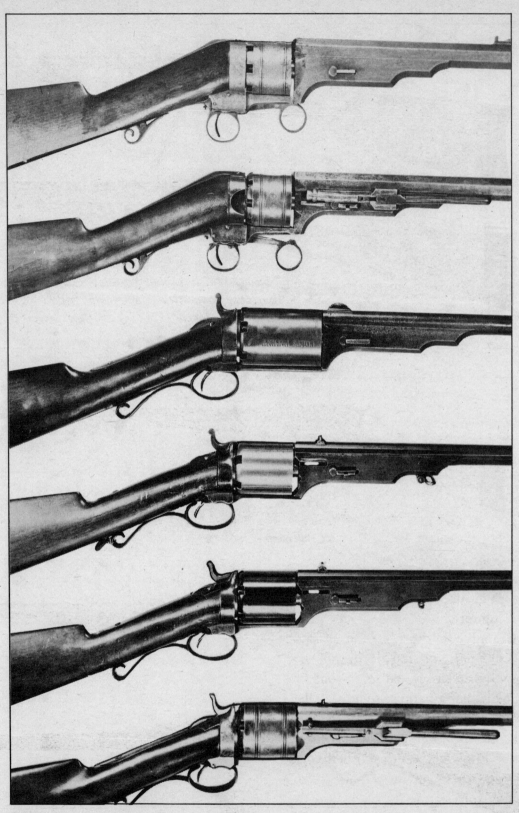

A variety of Colt 6- and 8-shot revolving shoulder arms made at Paterson, New Jersey. Third from the top is a shotgun.

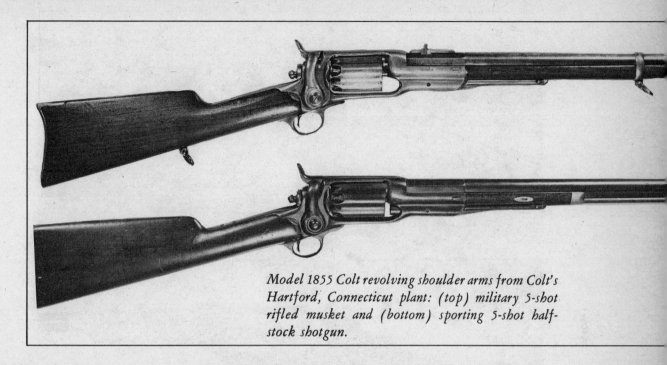

Model 1855 Colt revolving shoulder arms from Colt's Hartford, Connecticut plant: (top) military 5-shot rifled musket and (bottom) sporting 5-shot half-stock shotgun.

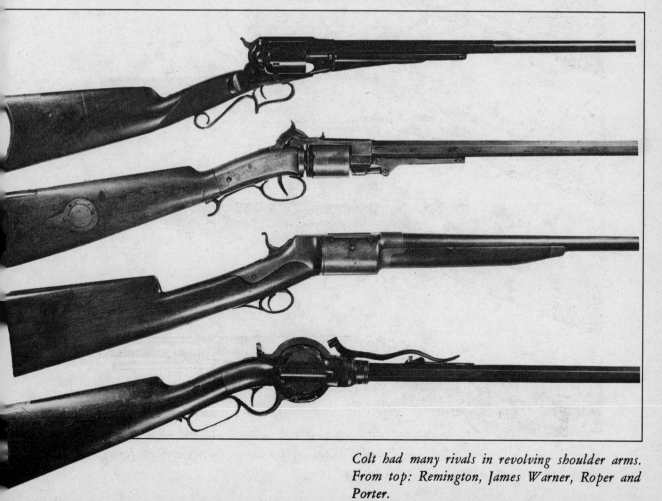

Colt had many rivals in revolving shoulder arms. From top: Remington, James Warner, Roper and Porter.

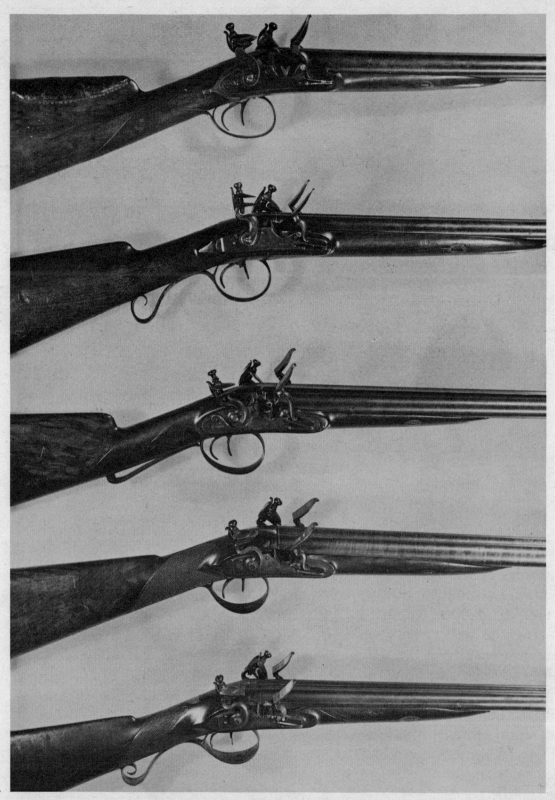

Imported arms were popular in the early 19th century just as they are today. Among the finest imports of the flintlock period were these double barrel English shotguns.

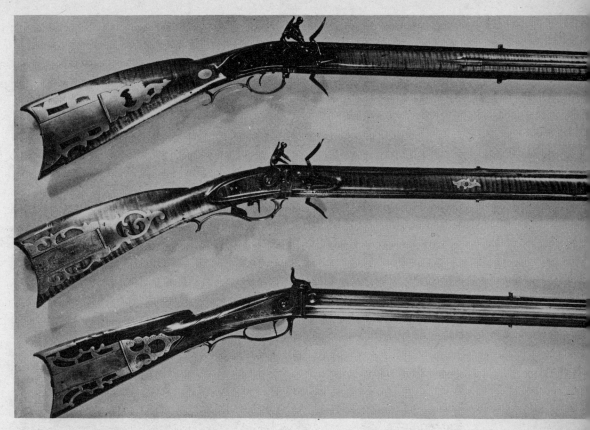

A few swivel-breech double barrel guns were made by various Kentucky riflemakers, but their muzzle-heaviness made them unpopular.

12-bore side-by-side double rifle, made by John Manton about 1780, exists. Quite expensive for their day, the few sold in America went mostly to well-to-do southern planters or prosperous merchants.

Some early effort was made at multi-shot flintlocks by the Pennsylvania gunsmiths, employing the European principle of over-under swiveling barrels, each with its own pan but fired by the same stationary lock. These guns proved to be rather clumsy and few were made.

CHAPTER TWELVE
The Gunmakers Move West

hifts in gunmaking activity occurred as New York, Ohio and the midwest became more settled. Gunmakers spread into these areas, the most notable in New York being Eliphalet Remington and his sons who built a plant at Ilion, a town served by the great Erie Canal.

In the early years Remington specialized in making barrels. Far wider activity lay ahead, however, and in 1845 the Remingtons received U.S. Government recognition—a contract to make breech-loading carbines on the patent held by William Jenks. These carbines, delivered to the Navy, are believed to have had the first drilled, cast-steel barrels (unwelded) ever supplied to the government. The Remington organization has gone on to become one of the giants in the American armsmaking field. Other gunmakers in New York state have made notable reputations also and I shall mention them as this outline progresses.

One of the most famous of the early 19th century gunsmith pioneers to head west was Jake Hawken, who went out to St. Louis when it was a far outpost of civilization. He was joined by his brother Sam in 1822, and thereafter the partnership of J. & S. Hawken was kept busy supplying the best caplock rifles available anywhere. Hawken rifles were used by the Mountain Men, guides, or anyone else venturing into the western prairies and mountains.

Fashions in gun stocks had undergone a change in these first few decades of the 1800s, and the traditional fullstock rifle had begun to be superseded by halfstock guns. Halfstocks were less liable to forestock damage and easier to make, yet took nothing from the accuracy or durability compared to the fullstock guns.

Hawken rifles were very sturdily built,

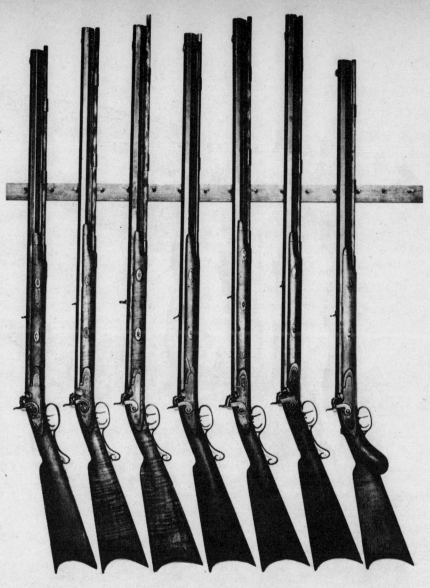

Favorites of Kit Carson, Jim Bridger and others who traveled the early West were these Hawken rifles. Made in St. Louis, Hawkens were equally deadly to a two-legged enemy or a four-legged beast.

having a halfstock with broad butt, plain iron fittings, and a strong rifled barrel averaging about 54 caliber. The locks were hand made and coupled with set triggers of special Hawken design. Hawken guns were capable of bringing down a buffalo, a grizzly bear, or a hostile Indian. Jim Bridger and Kit Carson used Hawken rifles extensively. Many expeditions to the West, including John Fremont's, stopped to outfit at the Hawken gunshop.

The Kentucky riflemakers in Pennsylvania and surrounding areas lost little time in adapting their guns to the caplock system and in converting flintlocks to use this advanced percussion ignition. They were doubtless among the first to provide the civilian trade with caplock hunting arms.

Up in New England, in this period between the War of 1812 and the Mexican War of 1846-1848, the gun manufactories had followed the lead of the government armories so much of their production up to 1840 continued to be the all-purpose flintlock smoothbore. However, a few gunmakers such as Allen, Leavitt, Cochran, Whittier and Nichols & Childs, had turned to the new caplock system. Samuel Colt was busy trying to sell

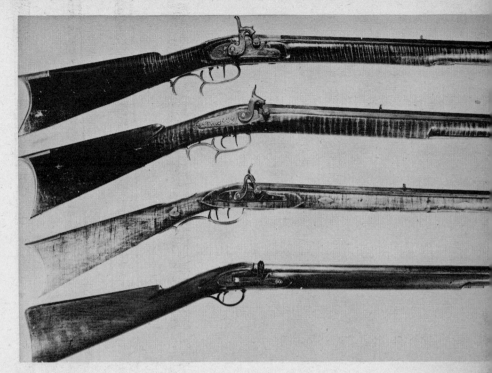

Variations in Kentuckys include (from top): bar action lock, back action lock, slim Bedford County lock and the mule-ear, sidehammer lock.

Close behind Sam Colt's 1836 patent were Nichols & Childs revolving cylinder pistol and the turret pistol by Cochran.

his new caplock revolving guns from his Paterson factory, but he was having a difficult time. Finally in 1842 the stock company manufacturing Colt's arms failed and Sam was out of a job. He was down but far from out and, with trouble brewing along the Rio Grande, his star was soon to be in the ascendency.

CHAPTER THIRTEEN
The War With Mexico

When the United States admitted Texas as the 28th state in late 1845, this was the spark which ignited the Mexican War. By then the United States had become of age. It had a reasonably substantial regular army and militia. Mounted troops such as the Dragoons were a fast-striking ground force, the Navy controlled our offshore waters, and immediately facing the Mexicans were very able fighting men known as the Texas Rangers.

The Mexican campaign was two-pronged. One force under General Zachary Taylor moved against Monterrey and General Winfield Scott captured Vera Cruz, penetrating into the heartland of Mexico. A second force had New Mexico and California as its objective. The U.S. Dragoons mounted up at Fort Leavenworth and started down the trail to Santa Fe. Both forces were destined to play a part in armsmaking evolution.

Some of the men heading into Mexico commanded by Generals Zachary Taylor and Winfield Scott still were armed with flintlock muskets. Others had the Model 1841 caplock rifles. It has always been a mystery to me why the government did not employ the sturdily built, well balanced Model 1841 54 caliber rifles for a longer period, and why they changed to the long 58 caliber rifled muskets in 1855 and 1861. Perhaps the larger-caliber rifled muskets were easier to load in the hands of inexperienced troops. In any case, the Model 1841 rifles became greatly popular in the West, where they were issued to emigrants, members of the Mormon Battalion, station attendants of the Pony Express and others. The same approximate caliber as the popular Hawken rifles, the Mississippi or "Jaeger" rifles as they were sometimes called were equally efficient against a two-legged enemy or a four-legged beast.

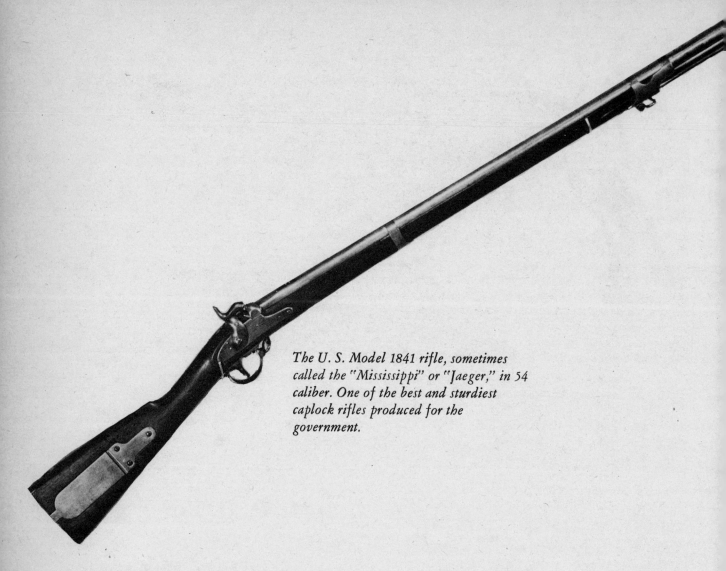

The U. S. Model 1841 rifle, sometimes called the "Mississippi" or "Jaeger," in 54 caliber. One of the best and sturdiest caplock rifles produced for the government.

As the war proceeded in Mexico, it became evident that better pistols were needed for mounted units who faced the Mexican lancers. A young former Texas Ranger named Samuel H. Walker, having transferred to the U.S. Mounted Riflemen, was selected to go north and find Samuel Colt to negotiate with him for production of a heavy repeating handgun on the principle of Colt's revolving arms made earlier at Paterson, New Jersey. The larger sized Colt's Paterson pistol, a 36 caliber model with a 7½ inch or 9 inch barrel, had been used both in the short-lived Texas Navy and in the Rangers with some success.

As a result of Walker's trip to Washington, a new model of Colt's revolver was designed and production started under a contract with Eli Whitney at his plant in Whitneyville, Connecticut. Colt had no manufacturing facilities of his own at that time. About 1100 pistols were produced. They weighed over 4 pounds, had a six-chambered cylinder, and a 9 inch barrel with a 44 caliber bore; collectors call them the Whitneyville-Walker Colt Dragoon pistol. They were produced during 1847 and reached Mexico late in the war, unfortunately too late for poor Walker—he had returned to duty and was killed during the

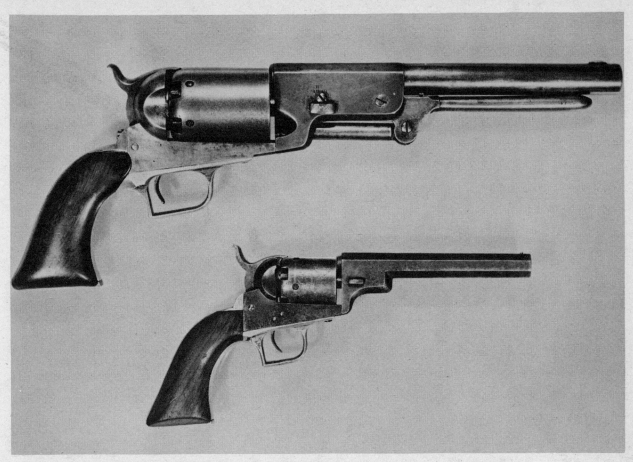

Colt's largest—and first truly successful—pistol was the "Whitneyville-Walker" used by the U.S. Dragoons in 1847. With a 9-inch barrel and weighing over four pounds, it is shown here compared to Colt's "Little Dragoon" Model 1848 pocket pistol.

capture of Huamantla in 1847. Of this brave, young 30-year-old soldier, his commanding officer wrote, "The victory is saddened by loss of one of the most chivalric, noble-hearted men that graced the profession of arms."

The immediate effect of the Whitneyville-Walker Colt Dragoon revolvers was that Samuel Colt was again in the arms business. He moved up to Hartford, opened a small shop to make revolvers, obtained some further government contracts, and the rest is history —another giant in the armsmaking field was born.

Back in the west, the U.S. Dragoons under General Stephen W. Kearny, armed with the breech-loading Hall caplock carbines made by Simeon North of Connecticut, big horse pistols and sabers rode into New Mexico. They took Santa Fe without resistance, left an occupying force there and, guided by Kit Carson, headed toward California.

After encountering stiff resistance from mounted Mexicans in the San Pascual Valley of California, the Dragoons fought through to San Diego. Here they joined with naval forces of the Pacific Squadron.

Most sailors and marines of the Pacific

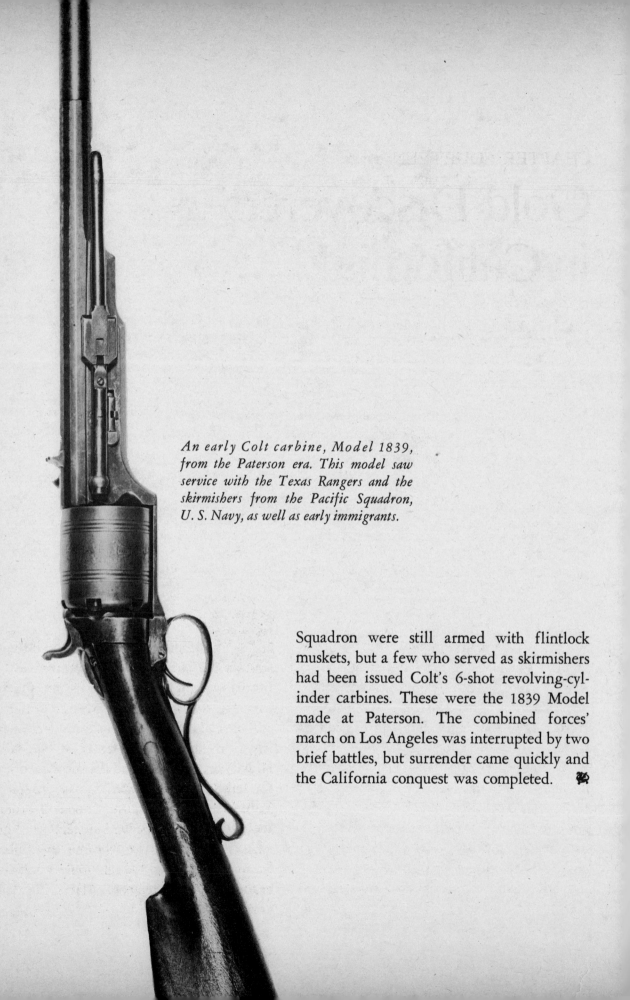

An early Colt carbine, Model 1839, from the Paterson era. This model saw service with the Texas Rangers and the skirmishers from the Pacific Squadron, U. S. Navy, as well as early immigrants.

Squadron were still armed with flintlock muskets, but a few who served as skirmishers had been issued Colt's 6-shot revolving-cylinder carbines. These were the 1839 Model made at Paterson. The combined forces' march on Los Angeles was interrupted by two brief battles, but surrender came quickly and the California conquest was completed.

CHAPTER FOURTEEN

Gold Discovered in California!

As the Mexican War headed toward a close, an event occurred in California which electrified the nation. On January 24, 1848 gold was discovered at Sutter's mill in Coloma. California came firmly into American hands by the treaty of Guadalupe Hidalgo in February, and the subsequent rush for land and gold led to a mass migration. Sailing ships and prairie schooners brought argonauts, merchants, land-seekers—and gunmakers. San Francisco became the hub of western gun trade, though some gunmakers headed out to Sacramento, Marysville, Lakeport and Coloma.

The Colt Navy Model and the Allen pepperbox, along with the Bowie knife, were as much a part of the 49er's kit as his gold pan and pumpkin-seed whiskey flask.

Indicating how brisk was the western arms activity, a few years ago I was able to compile a list of over 180 early California gunmakers. Among the leaders were Jules Bekeart, Benjamin Bigelow, Charles Slotterbek, Adolphus J. Plate, Nathaniel Curry, Claybrough & Golcher, and Horace Rowell. By the middle of the century we had established a vigorous arms-making trade on both coasts.

The western movement was a boon to all the nation's gunmakers, for no one ventured beyond the Mississippi and Missouri rivers without a good gun and possibly a pistol or two.

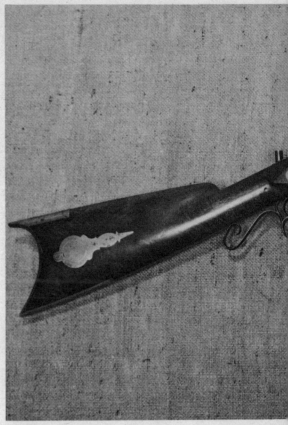

This group of California-made muzzle loaders, once part of the author's collection, includes single shot rifles, two and three barrel guns and a seven-shot cylinder rifle.

Piece by piece, by revolution, purchase or conquest, pieces of the jigsaw puzzle described by our various state lines began to fall in place. Venturesome Americans had pushed through the Cumberland Gap to the rich lands of Kentucky, down into the Southwest, into the Ohio valley, on to the great rivers that traverse the waist of the nation, into the prairies and—finally—through the mountainous divides to the coastal regions of the Pacific. Following this period of exploration came settled territories and then the states. It is doubtful that this all could have been accomplished in such a relatively short time without the gunmakers and their products in courageous hands.

The westward movement was not easy progress, before or after 1850. There would be 40 years of Indian warfare beyond the Mississippi and Missouri. There were signs of regional conflicts within the country, conflicts which were to lead to war between the states. Concurrently, in the theme of interest here, improvements were being made in the design, mechanical operation, and efficiency of firearms. This was still a period, however, dominated by the products of individual gunsmiths.

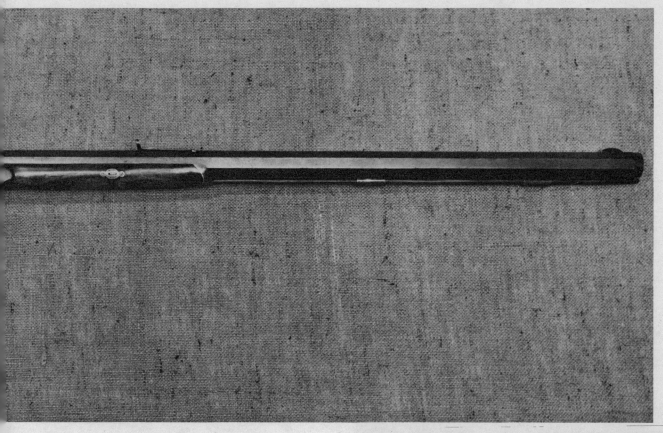

A typical California-made caplock rifle of the goldrush days. From the Edward Brown collection.

Often the smaller gunsmiths would buy assembled locks and partially finished barrels, assembling them into guns using stocks and fittings of their own design. Others were able to fashion entire rifles. It was inevitable that some individuals in the trade would excel others, and such individuals' fame spread. Leaving it to the larger gunmaking establishments to produce guns of specific models— as alike as peas in a pod—what may be called the "custom gunmakers" set out to produce arms of distinctive, personalized character for the discriminating civilian trade. 🐝

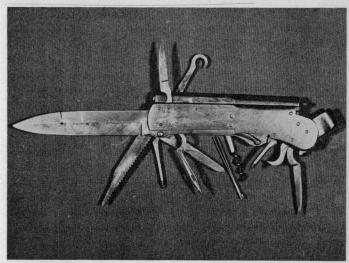

Some firearms designers concentrated on the bizarre —this multi-purpose knife also includes a caplock pistol.

CHAPTER FIFTEEN
American Marksmen Organize

merica's shooters took pride in their marksmanship, and starting with the "shooting at a mark" at Pennsylvania crossroads, the idea of formal shooting matches spread. In New York, New England, Pennsylvania, California and other sections too, target shooting became a serious business. Special target rifles having extra heavy barrels, tube or telescopic sights, special muzzles for precise loading and other features contributing to accuracy began to gain popularity.

New England had some great masters in this field, among them Norman Brockway, several members of the Whitmore family, and

Edwin Wesson. Edwin was the oldest of the three Wesson brothers, and his brothers Frank and Daniel were to become famous in their own right in separate armsmaking efforts.

Down in Philadelphia fine caplock match rifles were turned out by Kunz, Slotter, Wurfflein and a few others. L. W. Tisdel of Scranton made excellent rifles as did Horace Warner who worked at Williamsport, Pennsylvania and later at Syracuse, New York.

The New York gunmakers in this field were also a distinguished group, among them Morgan James, George Ferris, Nelson Lewis and William Billinghurst. Billinghurst was perhaps the most versatile of this group, making in addition to his excellent match rifles a rifle with a revolving 7-shot cylinder fired by percussion pills and a "buggy rifle" which was in effect a long barrel percussion pistol with an attachable shoulder stock.

The pill-lock system used by Billinghurst was a variation of the caplock. It employed the same kind of fulminate for ignition, but a little ball or pill of the detonating compound was placed in a hole in the breech and covered over with wax. At a blow of the special hammer-face the resulting fire was communicated through a vent to the loaded

This famous photograph was taken at the National Rifle Club of Vernon, Vermont, on the occasion of a spirited match to determine if Maynard breechloaders or heavy muzzleloaders were the more accurate. Norman Brockway, in shirtsleeves, championed the muzzleloaders while Arthur C. Gould, editor of Shooting & Fishing, standing fourth from right, championed the breechloaders' losing cause.

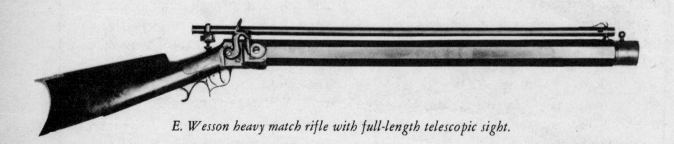

E. Wesson heavy match rifle with full-length telescopic sight.

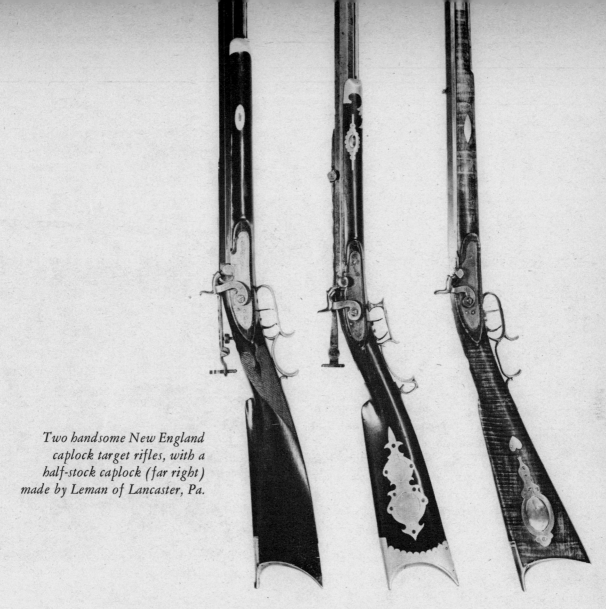

Two handsome New England caplock target rifles, with a half-stock caplock (far right) made by Leman of Lancaster, Pa.

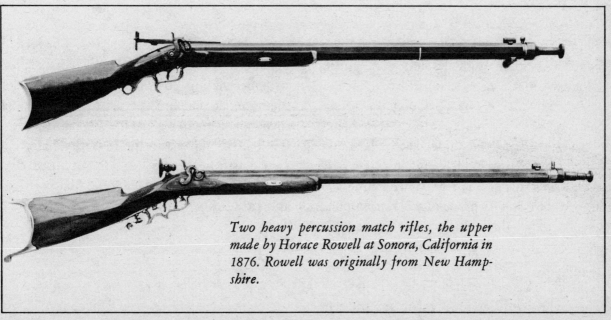

Two heavy percussion match rifles, the upper made by Horace Rowell at Sonora, California in 1876. Rowell was originally from New Hampshire.

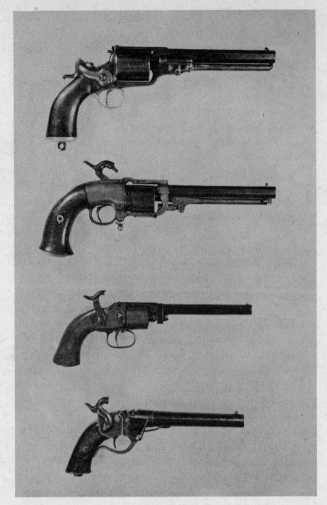

Four different makes of percussion revolver using automatically-fed ignition systems. The Rupertus (top), Butterfield (second), and Sharps (bottom) all used disc-fed systems. The Massachusetts Arms Co. model, second from bottom, used Maynard's tape ignition.

chamber to ignite the charge. The pill-lock was but another of the varieties of ignition systems used to fire a gun or pistol.

Dr. Edward Maynard, a dental surgeon, patented still another ignition system which was used in the U.S. Model 1855 rifled muskets, some Sharps models and in other rifles as well as in pistols. The Maynard primer was simply little lumps of detonating compound, spaced along a shellacked (waterproofed) paper tape, which was quite similar to the noise-making tape used in toy cap pistols.

Jesse Butterfield of Philadelphia was another who manufactured revolvers and der-ringer pistols to his own design. Butterfield invented a special lock from which discs filled with detonating compound were fed under the hammer. Jacob Rupertus of Philadelphia invented a revolver using detonating discs that fitted automatically into the hammer-face. Possibly the most extensively used disc ignition was that used in some Sharps rifles and carbines.

CHAPTER SIXTEEN

Christian Sharps' Breechloading Rifles

hristian Sharps was issued his first patent on September 12, 1848. This patent described a firearm with a dropping breechblock, making it one of the first breechloaders of the caplock period. The efforts of inventors during this period were directed toward several objectives—faster and easier loading, better ignition, and multi-shot systems. Christian Sharps had the first two of these objectives in mind when he had his first rifles made in the shop of A. S. Nippes at Mill Creek, Pennsylvania. These guns were fitted with an odd circular capping device, best described as a removable spring-activated

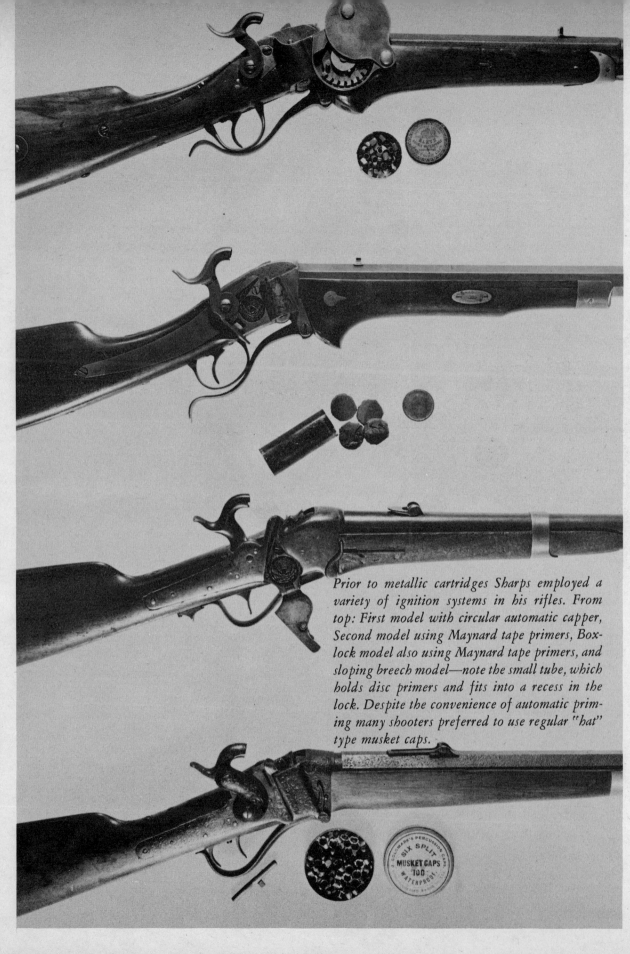

Prior to metallic cartridges Sharps employed a variety of ignition systems in his rifles. From top: First model with circular automatic capper, Second model using Maynard tape primers, Box-lock model also using Maynard tape primers, and sloping breech model—note the small tube, which holds disc primers and fits into a recess in the lock. Despite the convenience of automatic priming many shooters preferred to use regular "hat" type musket caps.

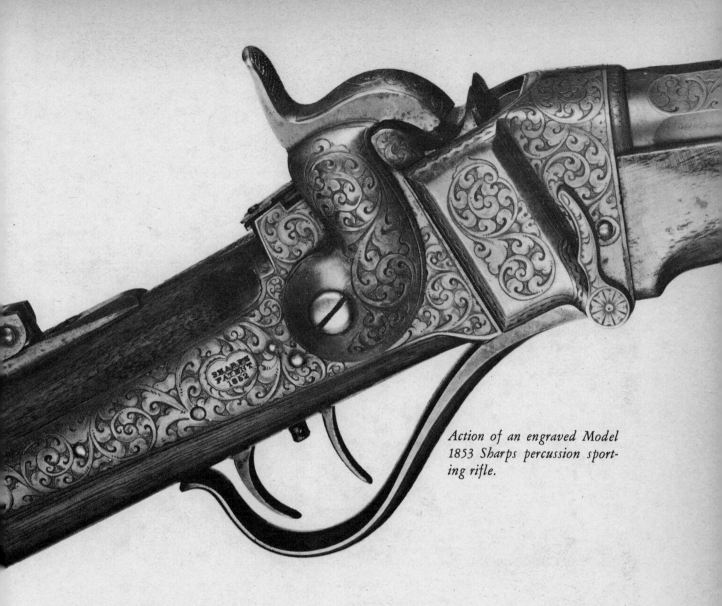

Action of an engraved Model 1853 Sharps percussion sporting rifle.

many-fingered wheel that revolved to feed individual percussion caps to the nipple. Not many were made and but few have survived. It was a priming system of dubious value, but a collector's item highly prized.

The second model Sharps rifle was designed with an entirely different automatic priming device, and we learn from the *Scientific American* of March 8, 1851, that "Albert S. Nippes & Co. have the exclusive right to apply Dr. Maynard's primer to the Sharps rifle, with the exception of the U.S. Government privilege to the same." For some reason Christian Sharps seemed obsessed

with the idea that to be a success his arms must be equipped with an automatic priming device.

Needing more capital, Sharps went to see friends in New England, to which a great concentration of arms manufacturing skills had gravitated. With the help of the Robbins & Lawrence firm at Windsor, Vermont, a stock company was formed at Hartford, Connecticut, which was known as The Sharps Rifle Manufacturing Company. Sharps was to serve merely as a technical advisor, with a royalty of one dollar per gun. In 1853 he returned to Philadelphia where he founded

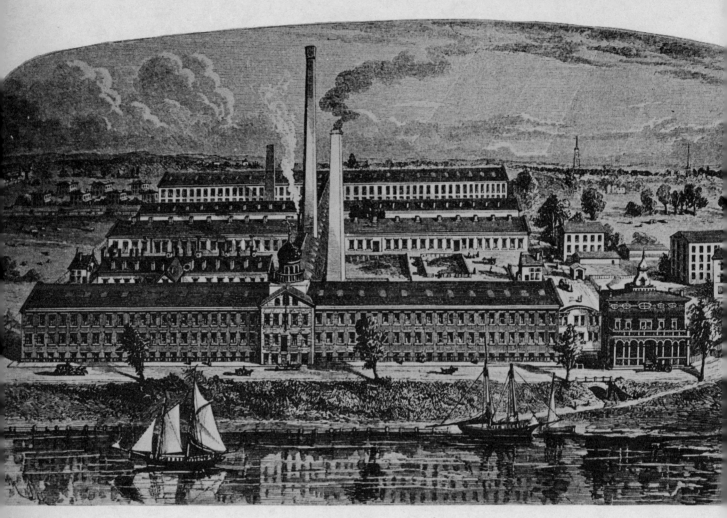

Colt's factory buildings along the Connecticut River grew in number to meet the expanding demand for Colt arms. Colt's plant became the largest industrial operation in Hartford.

C. Sharps & Co. and made some single shot pistols and light rifles, later producing four-barrel derringers.

The Sharps Rifle Manufacturing Company at Hartford, coming under the direction of the able Richard S. Lawrence, was launched on what was to become a distinguished career even though it was plagued, like so many arms companies, with the effects of recessions that endangered their financial structures. The Sharps factory in Hartford was but a stone's throw from the Colt factory. Thus it was that two famous names in arms-making were to be found in this one town

The Sharps Rifle Co. was another illustrious arms-making firm in Hartford. Here Sharps produced military, sporting and target arms before moving to Bridgeport.

on the Connecticut River, sandwiched between two other busy armsmaking towns of Springfield and New Haven.

As previously described, the early Sharps percussion carbines had a lock into which a column of discs could be inserted and—if all went well—fed automatically to the nipple. In practice, many shooters ignored the disc-feeding device and fired their Sharps with the dependable big copper "hat" percussion caps.

CHAPTER SEVENTEEN

The "Convertible" Pistol-Carbine

Among the experiments of the 1850s were efforts to develop an arm that could be used as either a pistol or as a carbine by attachment of a shoulder stock. This was not an idea unique to America, for it had been tried in Europe with somewhat mediocre success. However, it resulted in what was known as the U.S. Pistol-Carbine Model 1855 which was produced at Springfield Arsenal. The pistol was a big cumbersome model of 58 caliber with a lock designed for Dr. Maynard's tape primers. The coupling of the shoulder stock to the pistol was badly designed, and generally cracked the wood grip.

Somewhat better success with the pistol-carbine concept was had by Colt. Stocks with a three-point coupling were developed for use with Colt's big Dragoon pistols as well as the Navy and Army model pistols. A few of the stocks were even hollowed out to contain a metal canteen.

The idea of the pistol-carbine was a persistent one. Smith & Wesson, Stevens, Frank Wesson and others developed models, calling them "bicycle pistols" or "pocket rifles" as well as pistol-carbines. When the era of automatic pistols arrived some holsters were so designed that they could have a second use as an attachable shoulder stock. All a part of arms development, this was not one of its most successful ideas.

New England had taken a commanding lead in U.S. armsmaking as the 1860s rolled around. Samuel Colt was in active production, along with Sharps, in Hartford. An outgrowth of the short-lived production of Volcanic type arms in Norwich, Connecticut, was responsible for the foundation of Smith & Wesson in Springfield and for the New Haven Arms Co.—soon to become Winchester. Close to New Haven was the extensive arms factory of Eli Whitney.

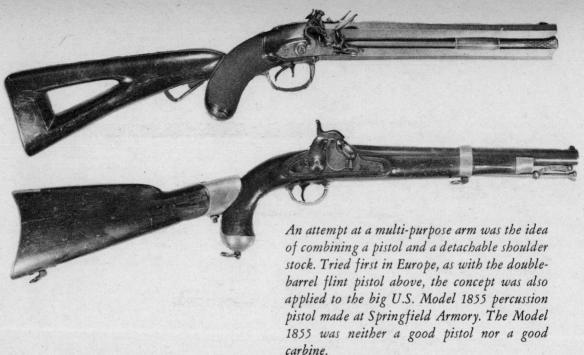

An attempt at a multi-purpose arm was the idea of combining a pistol and a detachable shoulder stock. Tried first in Europe, as with the double-barrel flint pistol above, the concept was also applied to the big U.S. Model 1855 percussion pistol made at Springfield Armory. The Model 1855 was neither a good pistol nor a good carbine.

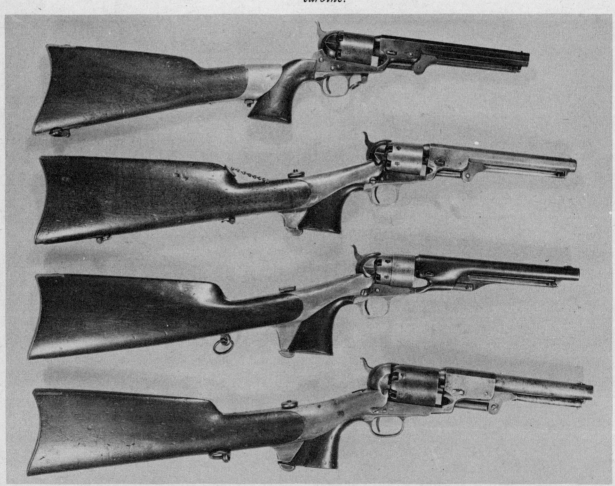

Colt also adapted the detachable shoulder stock to many models of his pistols. Shown here are two Model 1851 Navys, a Model 1860 Army and a Dragoon.

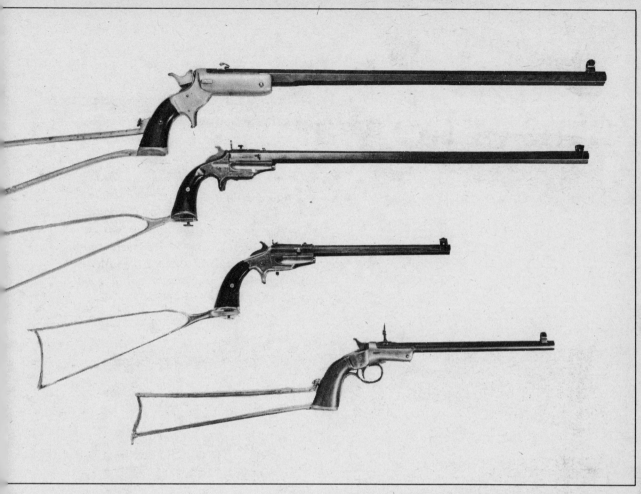

The detachable shoulder stock was probably most successful when applied to small caliber sporting arms such as these Stevens and Frank Wesson single shot pistols.

Springfield Armory was in active production in Springfield along with several private armsmaking establishments such as James Warner's, and in neighboring Chicopee Falls were the Massachusetts Arms Co. and the Ames factories. At Worcester, Frank Wesson's arms were made as well as those of Ballard, Ball, Greene and Allen. There were arms factories in every New England state, but the heaviest concentration was in the Connecticut valley. Such was the state of New England armsmaking as the echoes of the first hostilities at Fort Sumter died away and a call for increased arms production was sent out by the Federal and Confederate leaders.

CHAPTER EIGHTEEN

Arms of the War Between the States

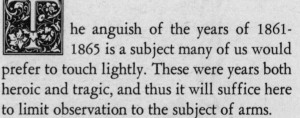he anguish of the years of 1861-1865 is a subject many of us would prefer to touch lightly. These were years both heroic and tragic, and thus it will suffice here to limit observation to the subject of arms.

Confederate forces were at a great disadvantage in the matter of arms supply. As the conflict began, most of their guns had come from the manufacturing plants in the North. Now they had to scramble for arms wherever they might be found. A rather amazing response was made, and small factories sprang into being from Virginia to Texas.

U.S. arms in southern arsenals were quickly

More soldiers carried Colts during the Civil War than any other maker's revolver. This Union soldier has a big four-pound Colt Dragoon tucked in his belt. Photo courtesy Herb Beck, Jr.

Among the most popular cap and ball revolvers of the Civil War were the (from top): Colt Model 1860 Army, Colt Model 1851 Navy, Remington, Starr single action, Starr double action, Savage and Allen & Wheelock.

Pistol makers proliferated during the War Between the States. These military revolvers include (from top): Butterfield, Rogers & Spencer, Joslyn, Freeman, LeMat, Pettengill Army and Pettengill Navy.

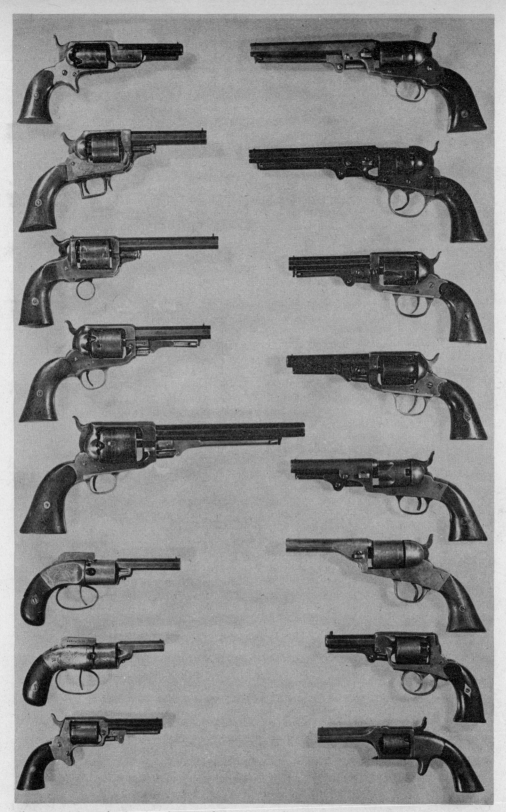

A great variety of other handgun makes were produced in the 1860s. Shown here are various models by Whitney, Ells, Bliss & Goodyear, Nepperhan, Cooper, Union Arms Co., Bacon and Sharps, only a sample of what was offered in this very competitive market.

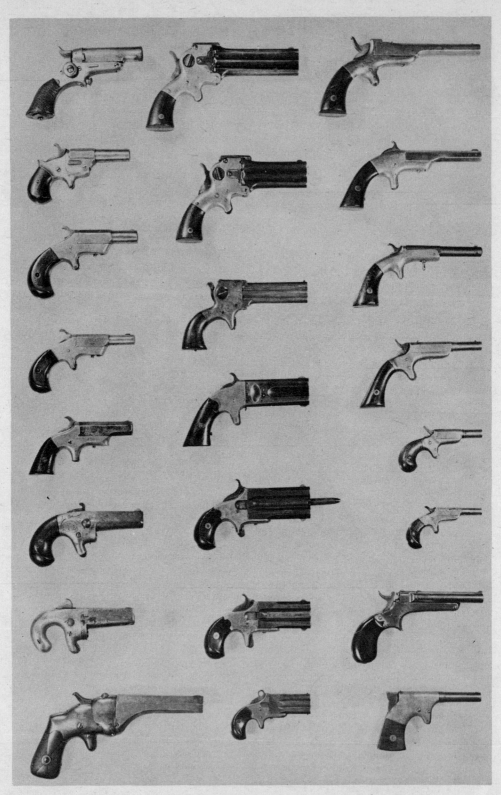

In addition to the wide variety of "standard" sidearms carried during the War Between the States, many soldiers also tucked a compact hand gun such as those shown above in boot or pocket.

SHAWK & McLANAHAN

T. W. COFER

TUCKER & SHERROD

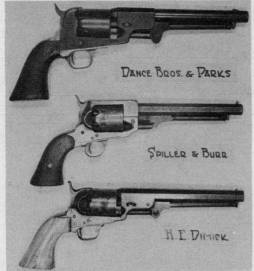

DANCE BROS. & PARKS

SPILLER & BURR

H. E. DIMICK

If anything, the armament of the Confederate forces presented even more variety than that of the Union. This group of Confederate pistols from the Carl Metzger collection at Texas A & M University is a good representation of handguns made in the South during the War Between the States.

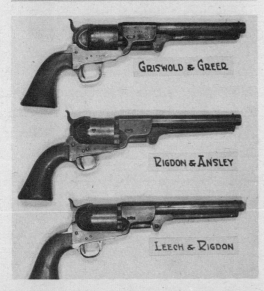

GRISWOLD & GREER

RIGDON & ANSLEY

LEECH & RIGDON

seized—for example those in the Harper's Ferry (Virginia) Armory, which had been partly destroyed by fire in a raid by followers of abolitionist John Brown in 1859. Emissaries were sent abroad by the South to buy arms wherever they could. It was a difficult task, but some English Enfield rifled muskets were obtained, as well as Austrian and other arms of various types.

The armory at Richmond responded well, as did the Palmetto Armory in Columbia, South Carolina. An overall coverage of all the many Confederate arms is too extensive to attempt a definitive review; while the arms may

During the War Between the States snipers sometimes used heavy, long-range match rifles with telescopic sights.

be relatively few in numbers, the shops in which they were made were numerous and the models were many and varied. When the war's end came there had been a great wasting of men and materiel and a long period of reconstruction lay ahead.

The shadows of impending war had been apparent long before hostilities began, and especially in the North many trials had been held to assess the value of new arms inventions. Many of the arms submitted to these trial were breechloaders; the subject is covered well in Claude Fuller's *The Breech-Loader in the Service.*

Unhappily, it took the holocaust of war to advance the efficiency of firearms. Two of the most noteworthy firearms improvements to come out of this conflict were the acceptance of metallic cartridges and the development of magazine-fed repeating rifles such as the Spencer and the Henry (New Haven Arms Co.). Hand arms benefitted, too, from the new self-contained metallic cartridges; Smith & Wesson pioneered the handgun field with 22 and 32 caliber rimfire models.

Lever-action arms were not especially new, but their employment of self-contained metallic ammunition was indeed a big step. In fact,

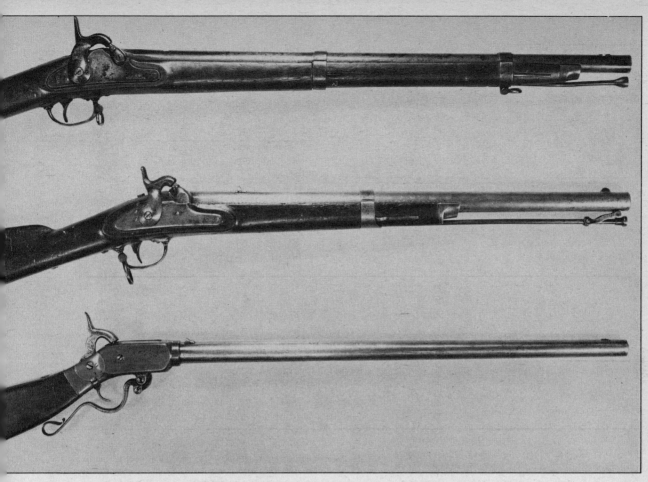

A variety of long guns were also produced by the Confederacy. Some representative examples are (from top): Richmond full-stock carbine, a C.S.A. conversion to carbine and a brass-frame C.S.A. model usually described by collectors as the Perry or Maynard model.

self-contained metallic ammunition was perhaps the greatest step forward in the management of a firearm since Dr. Forsyth's discovery of a detonating compound.

In 1848 Walter Hunt had patented a cartridge which was formed by hollowing out a cavity in a conical lead ball, filling it with powder and sealing the rear end with a priming disc. Starting out with a few Jennings rifles made at Windsor, Vermont, the Hunt type cartridges were employed next with some modification in lever-action, magazine-fed, repeating pistols. These arms were made on what was called a "Volcanic" system at

Norwich, Connecticut, by two bright young inventors named Horace Smith and Daniel B. Wesson. But their pioneer lever-action repeating pistols with the "Volcanic" ammunition, patented in 1854, did not catch the public fancy.

A new company named the Volcanic Repeating Arms Co. was formed in 1855. It was soon moved to New Haven where a well-to-do investor, Oliver Winchester, became interested. By 1857 the company was declared insolvent and Winchester, its largest creditor, gained control. The Volcanic patents led to formation of the New Haven Arms Co.,

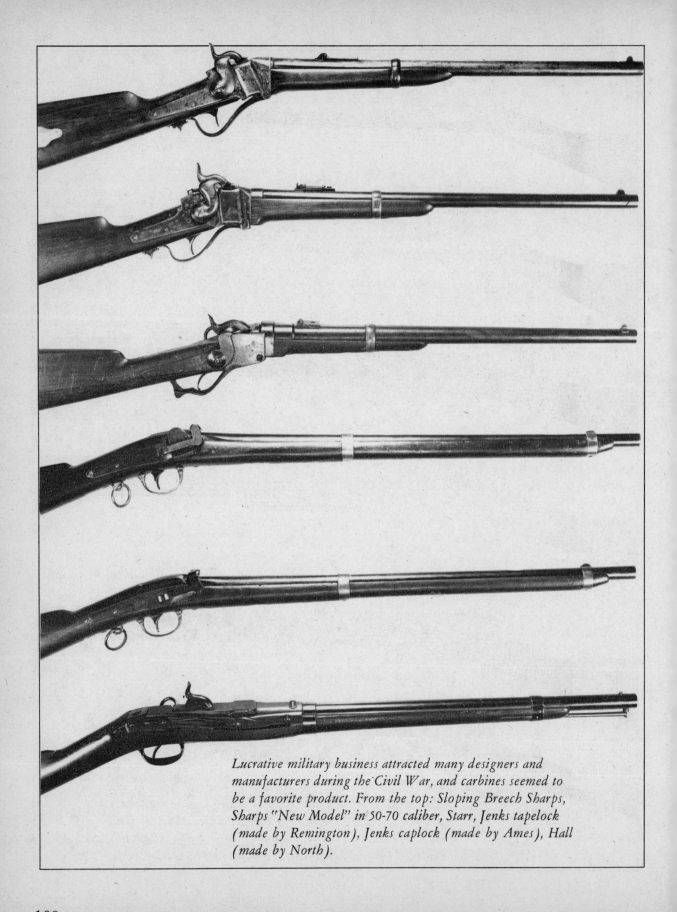

Lucrative military business attracted many designers and manufacturers during the Civil War, and carbines seemed to be a favorite product. From the top: Sloping Breech Sharps, Sharps "New Model" in 50-70 caliber, Starr, Jenks tapelock (made by Remington), Jenks caplock (made by Ames), Hall (made by North).

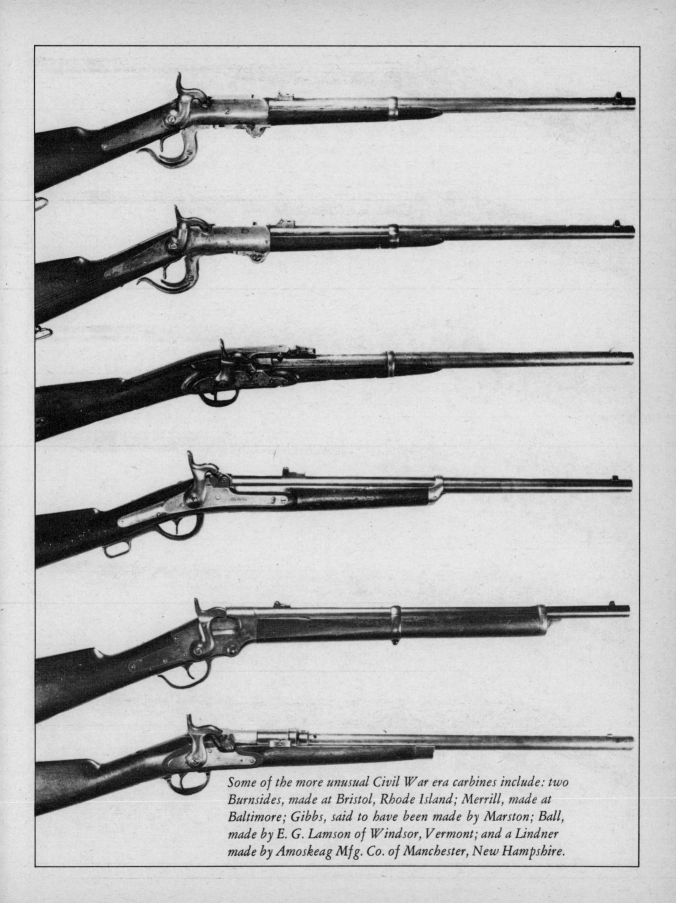

Some of the more unusual Civil War era carbines include: two Burnsides, made at Bristol, Rhode Island; Merrill, made at Baltimore; Gibbs, said to have been made by Marston; Ball, made by E. G. Lamson of Windsor, Vermont; and a Lindner made by Amoskeag Mfg. Co. of Manchester, New Hampshire.

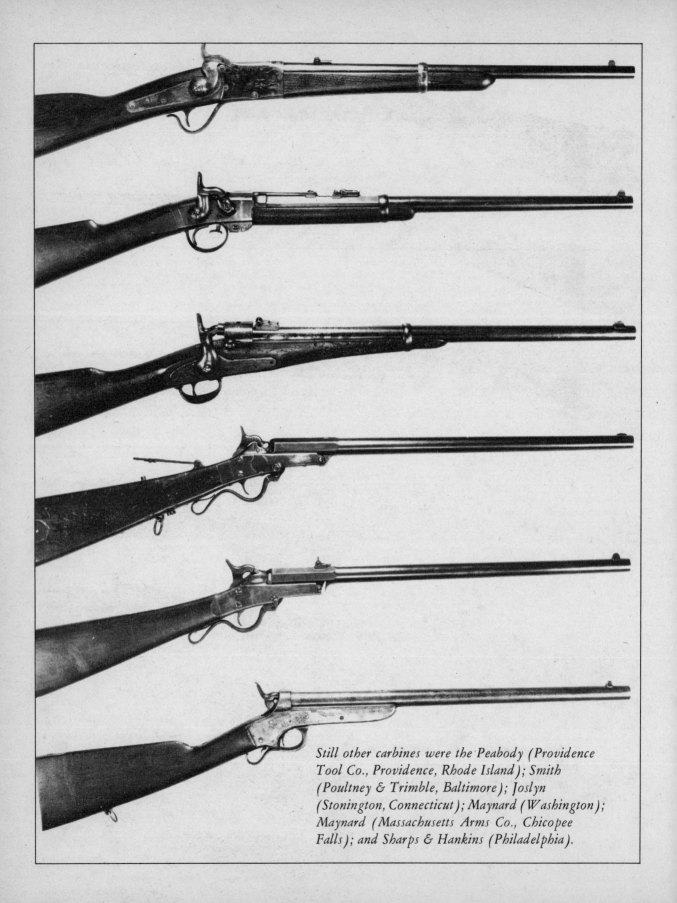

Still other carbines were the Peabody (Providence Tool Co., Providence, Rhode Island); Smith (Poultney & Trimble, Baltimore); Joslyn (Stonington, Connecticut); Maynard (Washington); Maynard (Massachusetts Arms Co., Chicopee Falls); and Sharps & Hankins (Philadelphia).

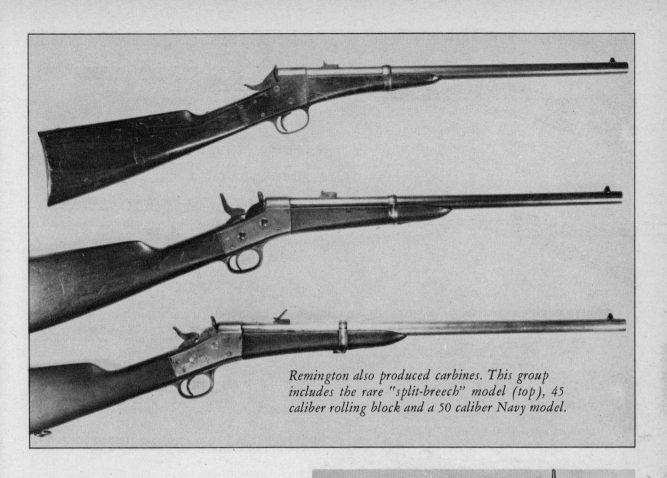

Remington also produced carbines. This group includes the rare "split-breech" model (top), 45 caliber rolling block and a 50 caliber Navy model.

Arms important in the evolutionary background of Winchester are (from top): Jennings single shot, Jennings repeater, Volcanic repeater, Henry 44 rimfire, Winchester Model 1866, Winchester Model 1873.

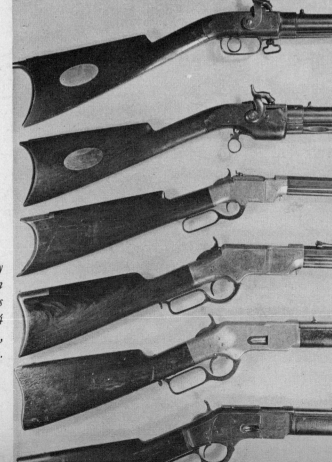

When Smith & Wesson's patents expired Colt tried a number of methods to convert their caplock revolvers to cartridge. A variety of Colt conversions are shown here.

which in 1860 produced the Henry rifle using a new 44 rimfire cartridge. A few years later the name was changed to Winchester Repeating Arms Co. and the first rifle bearing the Winchester name, the brass-frame 44 rimfire model of 1866, made its appearance. The Henry and somewhat less successful Spencer rimfire repeating rifles were the pioneers in shoulder arms employing self-contained metallic cartridges.

As any experienced cartridge collector will tell you, the variation in cartridges is almost endless. Starting with an attempt to simplify the old process of loading a gun with loose powder from a horn or flask and a ball from a bag of loose hand-moulded bullets, the first step forward came when the powder and ball were sealed together within a cylindrical paper or linen tube to form an easier-to-load cartridge.

This Henry rifle belonged to James Bunyan Hume, a native of New York who went west in 1850. He became a famous lawman in California and Nevada, and was for many years head of the Wells Fargo police. His Henry, which made the long trip from the Connecticut factory to California in 1864, saw a lot of history being made. Photo courtesy of the Wells Fargo Bank History Room.

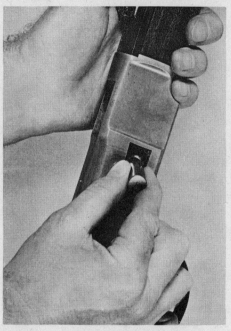

Loading a Model 1866 Winchester "Yellow Boy" with a 44 Henry rimfire cartridge.

The Henry repeating rifle had a front-loading magazine under the barrel that held 15 44-caliber rimfire cartridges. The competitive Spencer carbine was fed through a channel in the buttstock; its detachable tube magazine could hold seven 56-caliber cartridges.

CHAPTER NINETEEN

The Cartridge Comes of Age

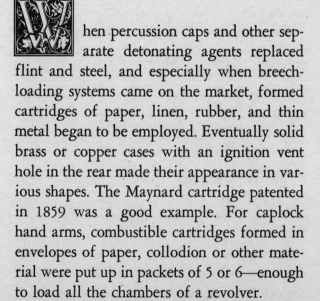hen percussion caps and other separate detonating agents replaced flint and steel, and especially when breechloading systems came on the market, formed cartridges of paper, linen, rubber, and thin metal began to be employed. Eventually solid brass or copper cases with an ignition vent hole in the rear made their appearance in various shapes. The Maynard cartridge patented in 1859 was a good example. For caplock hand arms, combustible cartridges formed in envelopes of paper, collodion or other material were put up in packets of 5 or 6—enough to load all the chambers of a revolver.

The advent of metallic cartridges called for the production of cartridge metal of copper and brass. In 1834 the Wolcottville Brass Company had been formed in Connecticut; the name was later changed to the Coe Brass Company. It was to them that most early cartridge manufacturers turned for cartridge case metal and a good measure of the success of those early cartridges might be traced to the admirable quality of the metal of which they were made.

Copper used in the manufacture of cartridge metal by Coe came from the Lake Superior region. Zinc in combination with copper for the manufacture of brass came from New Jersey and the Lehigh region of Pennsylvania. So great became the reputation of the Coe company that its brass was sold to Russia, Spain, Italy and Argentina. By 1880 Coe's production of cartridge metal alone mounted to 10 tons a day and called for the services of 300 workmen.

Improvement in the corrosion-resistant qualities of cartridge metal was achieved in 1876-1877 by Messrs. Leet & Chapin of Springfield, Massachusetts, by combining copper and brass. Tested by the U.S. Ordnance Department, their cartridge metal was

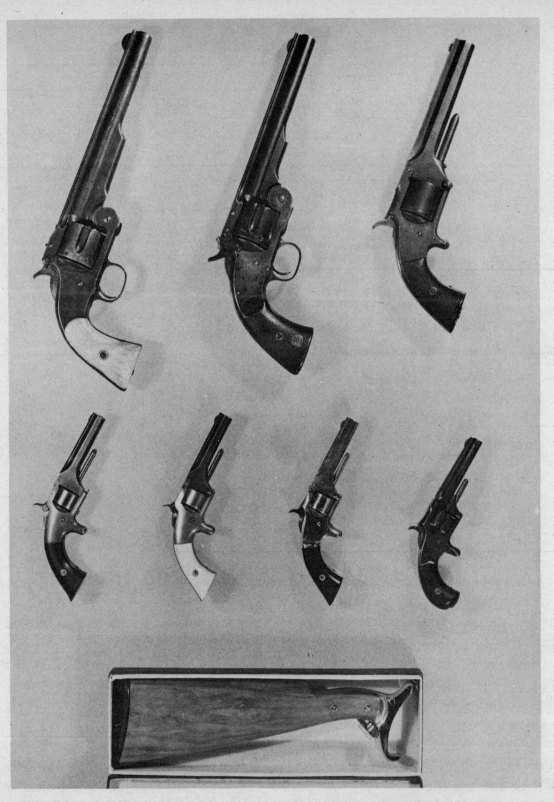

Pioneer in the cartridge pistol field, Smith & Wesson first made small tip-up barrel models in 22-caliber, then a 32 rimfire model (top right), and finally the big 44 top-break pistols. At the bottom is an accessory shoulder stock used with some later models.

Starting small in the early 1860s, Smith & Wesson's facilities were frequently expanded to meet the demand for their pistols.

found to retain the elastic qualities of brass, but was relatively resistant to corrosion.

With various metallic cases and patent self-contained ignition systems the variations were also great, going through pinfire, lip-fire, teat-fire; cup primer and other oddities. Two of the more extreme examples are the banded Crispin and the very strange Gallagher & Gladding with rounded rear and firing pin on the side.

The rimfire cartridge was the first really practical encased combination of primer, powder and bullet. Much credit must be given to Frankford Arsenal for the development

of this copper cartridge in military use, without taking anything from the early production of pistol ammunition by Smith & Wesson and rifle ammunition by Winchester.

Soon after the war, experiments with the new metallic ammunition led to conclusions that reloadable cartridge cases with an outside primer located in the center of the head would have important advantages. Widespread interest in cartridge production had led to formation of the Union Metallic Cartridge Company at Bridgeport, Connecticut in 1867 and the United States Cartridge Co. in Lowell, Massachusetts a year later. In addi-

A handsomely engraved New
Model Smith & Wesson. This
pistol, which was engraved and
gold inlaid by G. Young, was
awarded a medallion at the
World's Columbian
Exposition in Chicago in 1892.

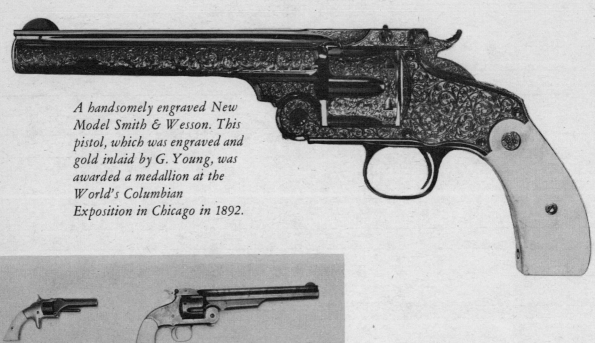

Smith & Wesson's product line
featured a wide variety of both
compact pocket models and
larger holster pistols.

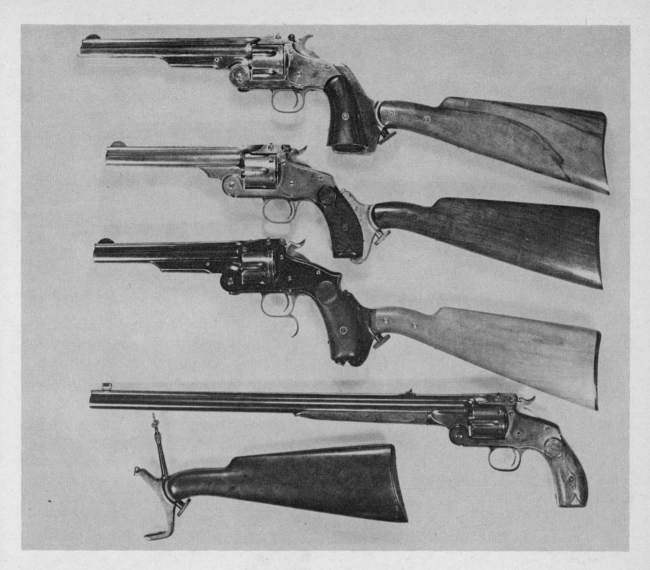

tion, Colt, Winchester and some other arms companies had established cartridge making facilities of their own. It was difficult at that time to visualize a Remington-UMC cartridge factory in Bridgeport (acquired by Remington in 1912) that would have over 300 buildings spread over 40 acres, or that other cartridge factories would expand in proportion.

Interesting Smith & Wesson accessories were the attachable shoulder stock shown here with some of the models with which they were used. From top: American Model, No. 3 New Model, Russian Model and Model 320 revolving rifle.

CHAPTER TWENTY

Western Growth Continues

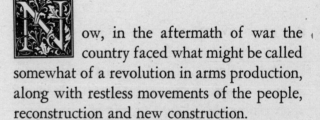ow, in the aftermath of war the country faced what might be called somewhat of a revolution in arms production, along with restless movements of the people, reconstruction and new construction.

Transportation and communications, restricted in growth during the war, gained new impetus. The telegraph line had been completed coast to coast, and on May 10, 1869, the tracks of the Central Pacific heading eastward met at Promontory, Utah, with the tracks of the westbound Union Pacific. Railroad access now would be vital to the nation's growth and especially to those areas between the great rivers and the Rocky Mountains, and on beyond to the Pacific slope.

We have learned that St. Louis had become an early crossroads for supply and migration. Soon places served by the railroad like Abilene, Wichita and Dodge City in Kansas, Denver in Colorado, Cheyenne in Wyoming, and Salt Lake City in Utah began to assume greater importance. In addition to the Union Pacific, rail lines of the Kansas Pacific and Santa Fe were also reaching westward.

Wagon trains had, of course, preceded the railroads. They opened the Santa Fe Trail, the Oregon Trail, the Bozeman Trail, the California Trail and the trails opened by Mormons to Salt Lake, and from Santa Fe to California by a para-military force known as "The Mormon Battalion" under Colonel Philip St. George Cooke.

Along these trails the army had built military posts to protect the emigrant and freighting wagon trains. Discoveries of gold in Montana in 1857-1863 and the gold rush to Colorado in 1859 contributed to the traffic westward and to the establishment of permanent settlements—and to Indian problems.

Denver was one of the first to become a vital supply town west of St. Louis and to en-

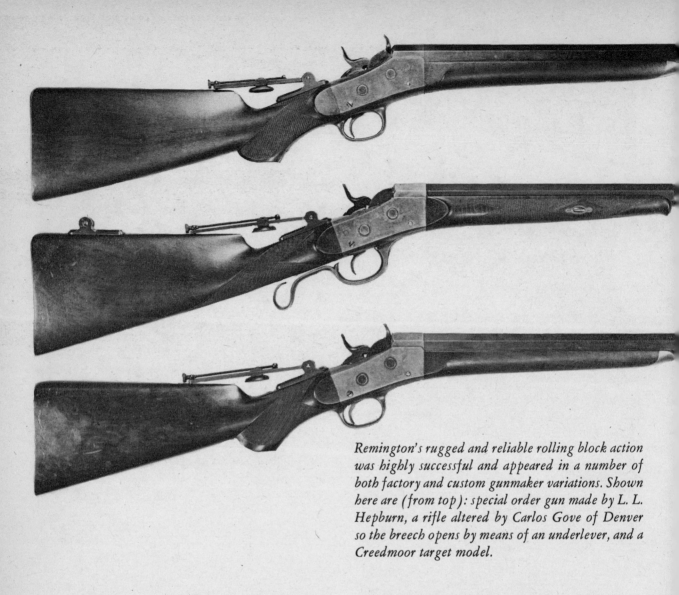

Remington's rugged and reliable rolling block action was highly successful and appeared in a number of both factory and custom gunmaker variations. Shown here are (from top): special order gun made by L. L. Hepburn, a rifle altered by Carlos Gove of Denver so the breech opens by means of an underlever, and a Creedmoor target model.

joy a prosperous growth as a result. One of the first gunsmiths to reach Denver was Carlos Gove, a tall, muscular native of New Hampshire. Having learned the gunsmithing trade as an apprentice in Boston, gunsmith Gove had also served a hitch as a Dragoon soldier and Indian fighter. Setting up a shop in 1862, Gove soon had a thriving business. Among those who served with him were John P. Lower and George C. Schoyen, both of whom were to make later history in the arms trade on their own. Among the innovations introduced by Carlos Gove was his design of an under-lever to open the breech of a Rem-

ington rolling-block arm instead of the factory thumb latch. Gunmaking in the early West was indeed an important and respected trade. As evidence of this, the record shows that Gove served as president of the fire and police board of the Denver city council.

East of Colorado a new movement was shaping up, too. By 1866 great herds of Texas cattle were heading up the trails to shipping points on the new railroads in Kansas. Down in Texas great herds of untended cattle had accumulated during the war. They represented a major cash crop for an area hard hit economically.

*Shown here (from top): a Creedmoor target model
and two heavy barrel big-bore hunting rifles.*

One of the first herds up the trail in 1866 in one of the longest of drives had as its destination the mining camps in Montana's Gallatin and Yellowstone valleys. Nelson Story, a young man who had mined in Montana and accumulated enough money to purchase a herd in Texas, was the leader of this drive. The route led northward to the Bozeman Trail, also known as the "Trail of the Fighting Sioux." It was well named for, as Story's herd snaked its way between Fort Laramie and Fort Reno, a band of Sioux Indians swooped down on the herd from behind concealing hills, cut off a small segment and drove the animals back behind the hills at a rapid pace.

Nelson Story was not one to give up anything that was his without a fight—and he had an ace up his sleeve. In his wagon was a case of Remington "rolling-block" rifles, among the very first breechloaders to come out to the prairies. Breaking out the rifles and their 50 caliber ammunition, Story and his Texas drovers set out in pursuit.

Grown careless by their apparent easy success, the Indians had stopped to butcher a cow for a big feast. With quick vengeance Story and his men descended upon them with guns

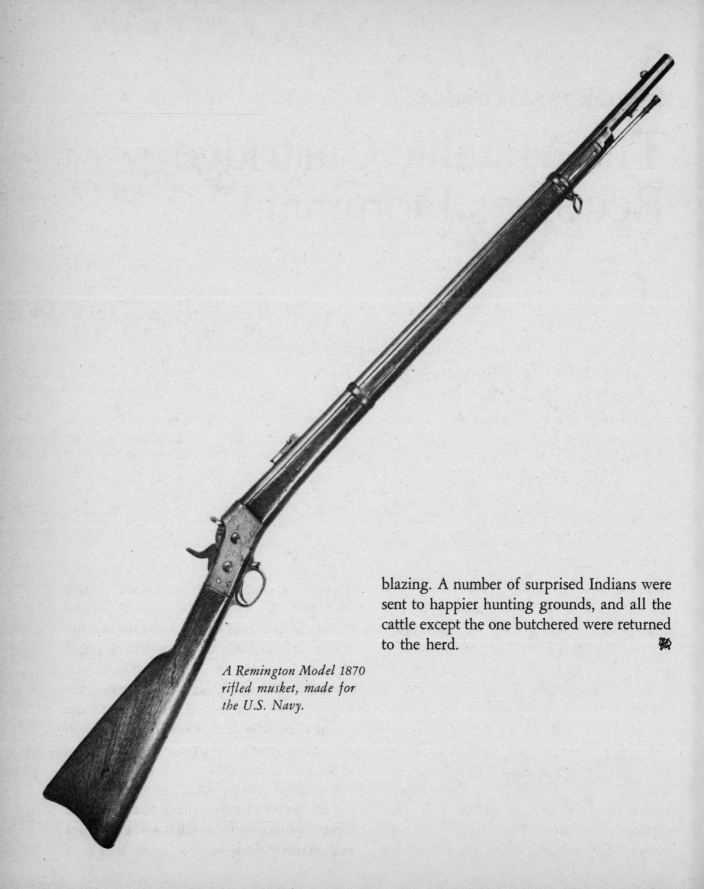

A Remington Model 1870 rifled musket, made for the U.S. Navy.

blazing. A number of surprised Indians were sent to happier hunting grounds, and all the cattle except the one butchered were returned to the herd.

CHAPTER TWENTY-ONE

The Metallic Cartridge Becomes Dominant

emington's "rolling-block" single shot breechloaders were to become one of the most famous and widely used rifles of the following decades. They shared popularity with the Sharps in the buffalo harvest and in the first international shooting matches at Creedmoor. Further, they soon came to be used by the Danish, Swedish, Spanish, Mexican, Egyptian and other military forces as well as the U.S. Army, Navy and militia. Production of these uncomplicated, strong rifles, in a great variety of calibers and types, kept the wheels turning busily in the Remington plant at Ilion, New York.

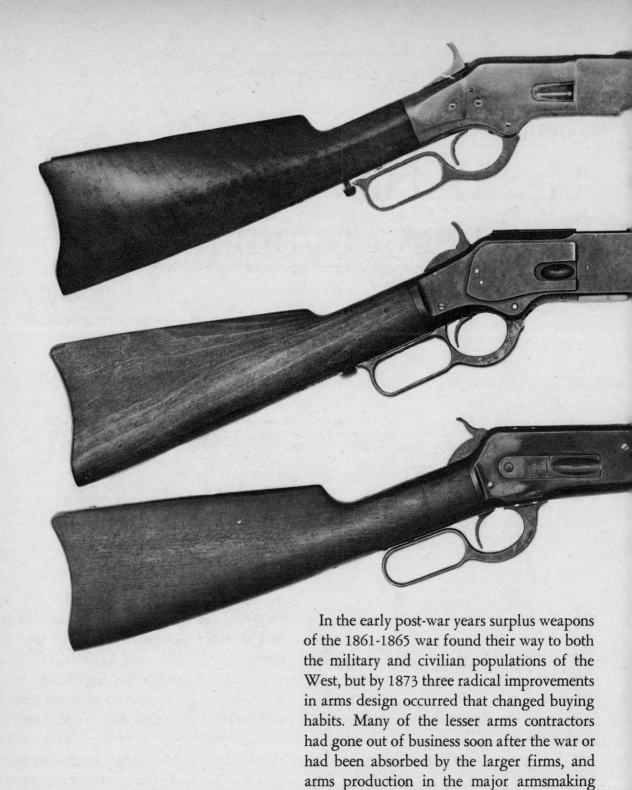

In the early post-war years surplus weapons of the 1861-1865 war found their way to both the military and civilian populations of the West, but by 1873 three radical improvements in arms design occurred that changed buying habits. Many of the lesser arms contractors had gone out of business soon after the war or had been absorbed by the larger firms, and arms production in the major armsmaking plants underwent the change-over from military weapons to guns more suited to civilian trade. The Spencer Repeating Rifle Co. of Boston was one of the major firms that failed. In 1869 Spencer's plant was sold at auction

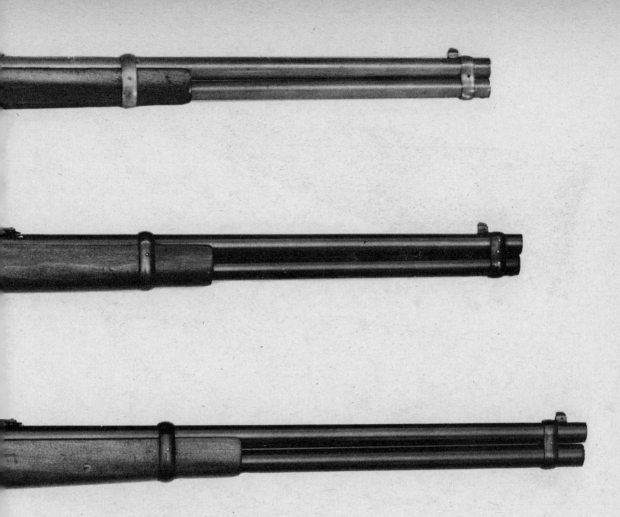

The three Winchesters that helped win the West. From top, Model 1866, Model 1873 and Model 1886.

and absorbed by the Winchester Repeating Arms Co.

Winchester had come out of the war in good shape. A pioneer in lever-action repeating rifles using metallic cartridges, in 1873 they redesigned their rifles, using iron receivers instead of brass, and introducing a new 44-40 W.C.F. (Winchester Center-Fire) cartridge. This rifle, like the Remington rolling-block, was destined to become one of the most popular models ever produced. More powerful than the old 44 rimfire models, and with reloadable cartridge cases, its appeal was so great that by the time it was officially discontinued

in 1919 the records showed that 720,610 Model 1873s had been made, sold and delivered.

Carbines, sporting rifles and military muskets were offered in this model, and available calibers eventually ranged from the 22 rimfire through the 32-20, 38-40 and 44-40 Winchester center-fire cartridges. Some especially accurate guns were fitted with nicely grained stocks, given a bit of engraving and marked on the barrel "1 of 1000" or "One of One Thousand." Guns so treated are today a valuable prize for collectors.

The Model 1873 Winchester was only one

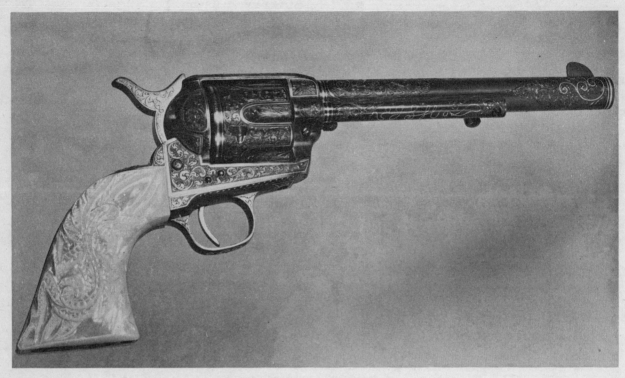

One of the most popular handguns of all time was the Colt Single Action Army. This handsome example was engraved by Alvin A. White and inlaid with gold and platinum. Photo courtesy William L. Rogoski.

of the great advances in arms design of that year. Up the river at Hartford, Colt had a surprise of its own in what we have come to know as the Model 1873 Colt Single Action Army revolver. First chambered for the 45 Colt centerfire cartridge, it was later chambered for the Winchester 32-20, 38-40 and 44-40 calibers. A few were even made in 22 and 44 rimfire chambering. Later, single actions chambered for a number of more modern cartridges such as the 38 Special were made available, as well as various foreign cartridges. In the 44-40 caliber the revolver was called the "Frontier Six-Shooter"; in 45

this single-action model was popularly called a "Peacemaker." It gained almost immediate popularity and its manufacture is continued to this day, not only by Colt but by other manufacturers, Colt's patents having long since expired.

CHAPTER TWENTY-TWO

Indian Fighting With the Trap-Door Springfield

hird in the 1873 popularity parade was a military arm produced at Springfield Armory. This gun was the outgrowth of the government's many experiments with systems to convert quantities of their old rifled muskets from muzzleloaders to breechloaders. The system found most practicable consisted of a hinged breech atop the rear of the barrel fastened by a latch; it was designed by E. S. Allin, the master armorer of the Springfield Armory. First conversion efforts in 1865 were less than promising but in 1866 a better design was accomplished which included a tube brazed inside the old 58 bore

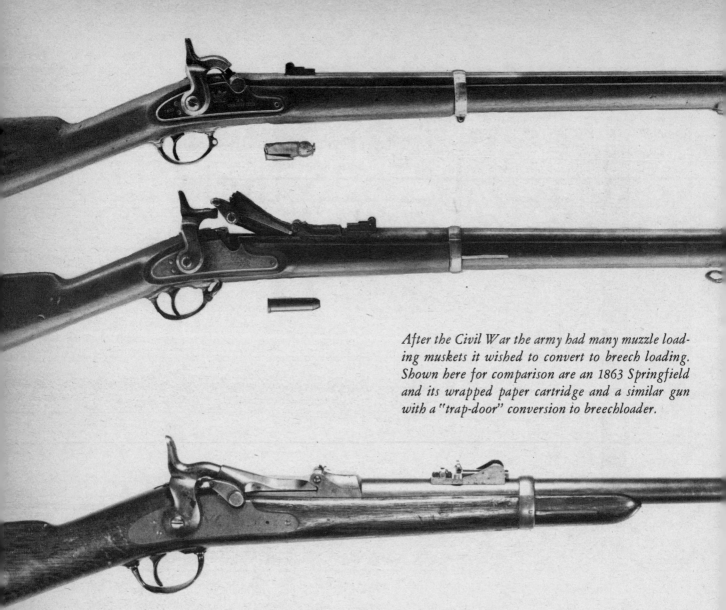

After the Civil War the army had many muzzle loading muskets it wished to convert to breech loading. Shown here for comparison are an 1863 Springfield and its wrapped paper cartridge and a similar gun with a "trap-door" conversion to breechloader.

The trap-door conversion eventually became the standard U.S. Army rifle in 45-70 caliber. Shown here is a Model 1873 carbine.

barrel to make the gun suited for the new 50-70 cartridges. By 1868 the receivers became a separate unit into which a new barrel was screwed.

Finally, having gone through various improvements in the breech mechanism and elsewhere and with the bore reduced to chamber the new 45-70 cartridge, the Springfield rifle emerged as the "Model 1873."

Originally produced as a U.S. carbine, cadet rifle, and full-length rifle, additional models later included a fullstock carbine, an engraved officer's model, a shotgun, and a hunter's model with octagon barrel.

Among the rarest of the many "trap-door" Springfield variations are the Officer's Model (top) and the special octagon barreled "Hunter's Models."

Detail of the action of an Officer's Model 1873 Springfield.

Among the interesting accouterments of the Model 1873 were a sliding rod bayonet and a trowel (entrenching) bayonet as well as the standard triangular type.

Some of the early 50-70 converted Springfield rifles were used effectively by soldiers from Fort Phil Kearny at the Wagon Box fight in Montana. Buffalo Bill Cody used a 50-70 he fondly called "Lucretia Borgia" to down 4000 buffaloes when he was employed to furnish meat for workers on the Kansas Pacific Railroad. It was the Model 1873, however, that played a major role in the Indian wars. The 7th Cavalry and other U.S. units were

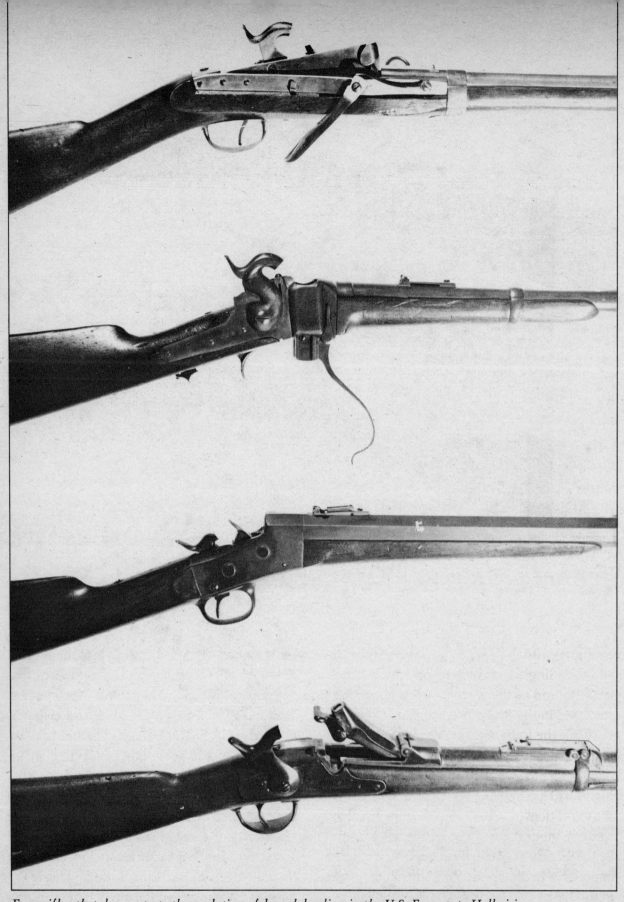

Four rifles that demonstrate the evolution of breech-loading in the U.S. From top, Hall rising block, Sharps dropping block, Remington rolling block and the hinged Springfield "trap-door" block.

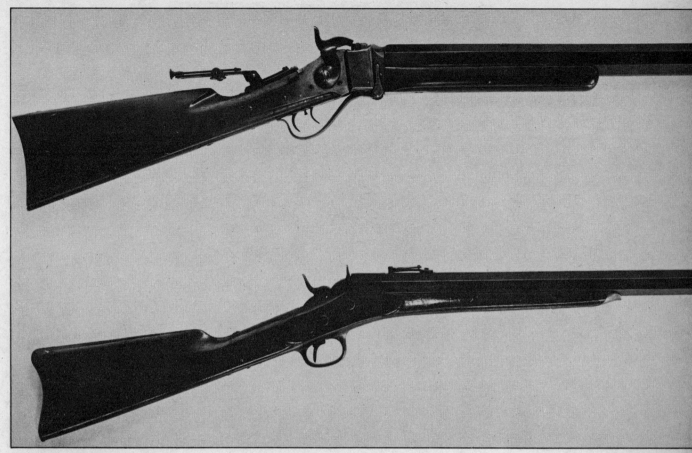

*The two most popular big bore rifles for buffalo hunting were
the Sharps and the Remington shown below it.*

equipped with Model 1873 carbines and rifles
and Colt Single Action Army revolvers almost
until the end of the century, when a few were
still used in the Spanish-American War.

While the Indian wars raged from the Cana-
dian border to the Mexican border between
the Rocky Mountains and the Mississippi and
Missouri rivers in the 1870s and 1880s, with
the exception of a few custom guns made by
western gunmakers, most of the guns found
in the hands of Americans and their Indian
opponents had come from gunmaking plants
in the East.

The government's reservation plan for the
Indians had included supplying them with
guns. By gift, trade, or theft the Indians had
obtained flintlock "Northwest" trade guns,
some caplock Leman rifles made in Lancaster,
Pennsylvania, Sharps rifles and carbines, a few
Henry rifles and some other effective weapons. The arms of the U.S. soldiers were now
cartridge arms, produced in eastern arms factories. Even in California it had become more
practical and economical to import cartridge
arms from the big factories in the East than
to make them in small local shops. Hence the
various gunsmiths turned their hands mostly
to repair and occasionally to converting guns

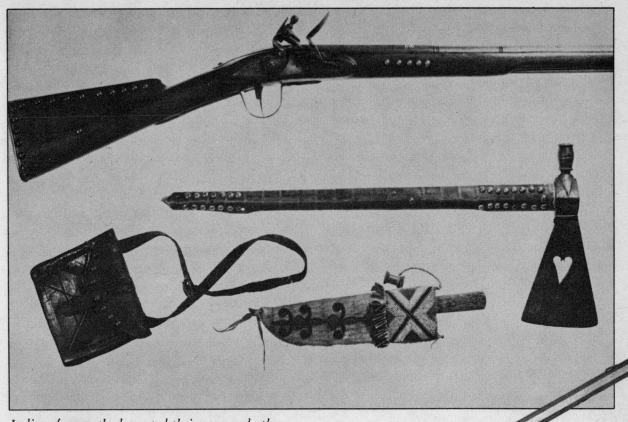

Indians frequently decorated their guns and other equipment with brass tacks. Shown here are a standard "Northwest Gun" and pipe tomahawk, along with a bag for accessories and a sturdy knife.

(Facing page.) One of the best-known Indians of the western Indian wars was Geronimo, war chief of the Apaches, shown here with what is probably a Springfield carbine. Courtesy Smithsonian Institution.

Indian guns suffered rough treatment—note the battered buttstock and rawhide fore-end repair on this H. E. Leman caplock.

to the newer ignition systems. A. J. Plate purchased a large number of the old Spencer carbine actions, fitted them with new octagon barrels, and made hunting guns of them. It had become a time now for the emergence of big arms distributors and such establishments were to be found in Boston, New York City, Philadelphia, Cincinnati, St. Louis, Denver and San Francisco.

CHAPTER TWENTY-THREE
Serving the Civilian Market

or a time at least thoughts had turned from war in the East and Far West, ushering in a period during the 1870s when sporting and target guns and pocket pistols were given special attention. With the advent of the small 22, 32, 38 and 41 rimfire cartridges many plants blossomed out with small pocket pistols, following Smith & Wesson's lead and especially after the Smith & Wesson patents expired in 1869. Colt, Remington, Stevens, Sharps, Allen, Starr and others offered a number of models. Single shot cartridge derringers and cheap revolvers came from plants never heard of before—many active only a short time. Some of these pistols and revolvers employed such odd cartridges as the teat-fire and lip-fire, mentioned earlier, but most were chambered for the more conventional rimfires. The better single shot derringers showed a preference for the rimfire 41 caliber. In this period also appeared oddities in pistol design now classed as "firearms curiosa." Included were palm pistols, knife pistols, knucks pistols, harmonica-shaped pistols and others, few offering anything more than novelty.

Police handguns, designed as such, now were offered, Colt even producing a pistol with a raised "cop and thug" design in the hard rubber stocks. Double-action models became popular. So it was that a plethora of small handguns was produced, with demand mostly in the cities and towns. The West held to its big 44 or 45 six-shooters such as the Colt, Smith & Wesson, Remington and Merwin & Hulbert revolvers (made by Hopkins & Allen).

Another side to armsmaking was also coming on the scene as the 1870s rolled along. Significantly, the National Rifle Association had been formed in 1871 to encourage, among other things, an improvement in marksman-

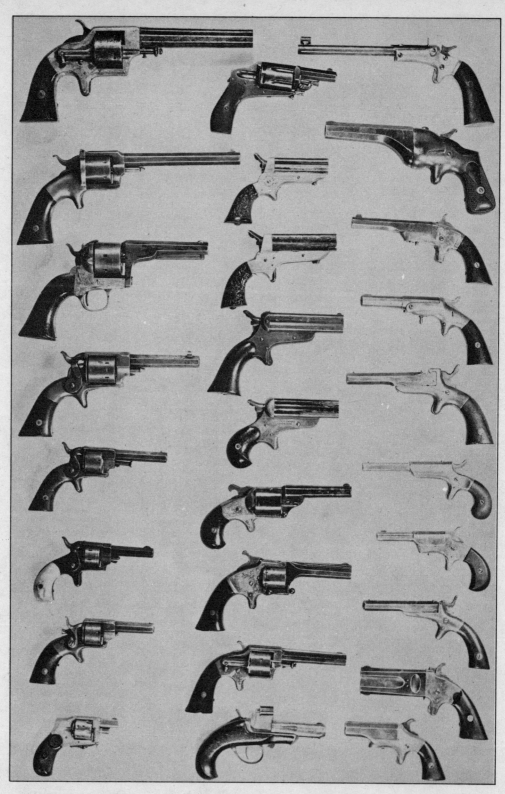

Among this group of pistols from the early years of the metallic cartridge era are to be found cup-primer, lip-fire, teat-fire and rimfire models in various calibers, capacities, sizes and shapes.

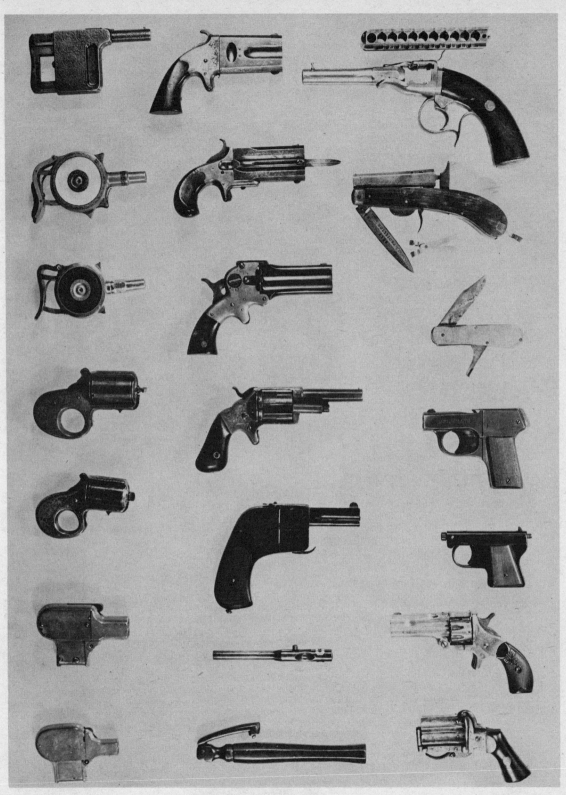

Many unusual designs were offered during the late 19th century as inventors attempted to combine compactness, convenience and capacity.

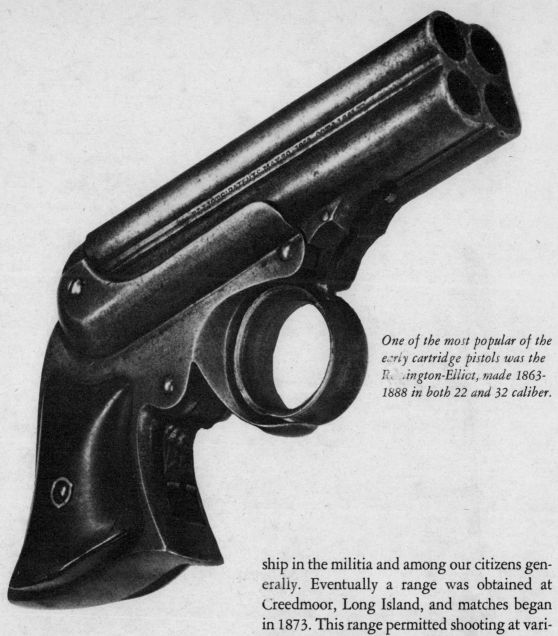

One of the most popular of the early cartridge pistols was the Remington-Elliot, made 1863-1888 in both 22 and 32 caliber.

ship in the militia and among our citizens generally. Eventually a range was obtained at Creedmoor, Long Island, and matches began in 1873. This range permitted shooting at various distances up to 1000 yards. The rifles used at first were military arms such as the Springfield hinged-breech or "trapdoor" rifles, the Remington rolling-block 50 caliber guns and a few others.

In 1873 the Irish Rifle Team won the Elcho Shield, symbolic of the rifle championship of the British Isles. They were anxious to challenge the world to demonstrate their marksmanship superiority. Although they regarded

Shooting clubs proliferated—here the Champion Gun Club Team of Arizona, circa 1894.

Early dress of the cowboy inevitably included a holstered six-shooter.

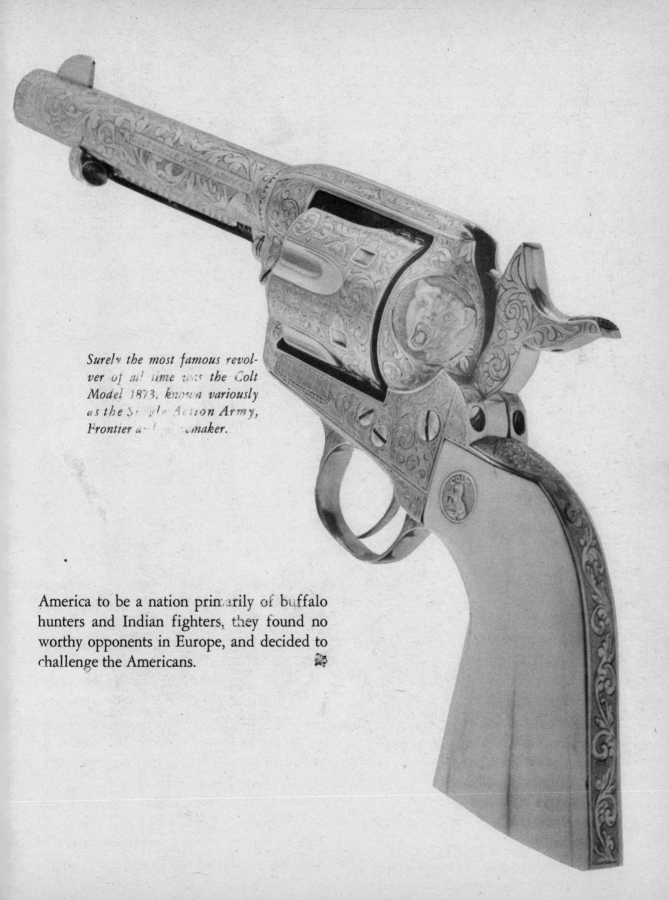

Surely the most famous revolver of all time was the Colt Model 1873, known variously as the Single Action Army, Frontier and Peacemaker.

America to be a nation primarily of buffalo hunters and Indian fighters, they found no worthy opponents in Europe, and decided to challenge the Americans.

CHAPTER TWENTY-FOUR
America's Marksmen Go International

assing quickly over the details, the two national teams met at Creedmoor, the first shots booming away on September 26, 1874. The result was a great and somewhat unexpected victory for the Americans, the score 934 to 931. Important in this victory were the specially built "Creedmoor" long range rifles made for the American team by E. Remington & Sons under the supervision of L. L. Hepburn, and the Sharps rifles prepared by that company's best craftsmen under G. W. Yale.

Here, indeed, was a great step toward regular production of beautifully made single shot target rifles, and even fine single shot rifles of the plainer hunting type. Similar to the enthusiasm of American collectors of Kentucky rifles, which has led to the formation of the Kentucky Rifle Association, and the great interest in martial arms which has led to formation of the Company of Military Collectors and Historians, the qualities of single shot rifles have inspired formation of the American Single Shot Rifle Association. Specific interests draw many enthusiastic supporters.

The manufacture of fine quality American rifles and pistols having reached a point of notable accomplishment by the early 1870s, a closer look on how this was accomplished may be helpful. Perhaps in simplest terms it may be attributed to American inventive and mechanical genius along with skilled craftsmanship.

Hand tools had been replaced in most operations by the increasing use of machinery, in which great advances had been made. American inventors had no superiors and very few equals in this field. One of the first big steps toward making gun manufacture easier and more uniform was the Blanchard stock-turning machine developed at Springfield Armory. Pratt & Whitney of Hartford were among the leaders in producing gun machinery, devoting

Scene at the Creedmoor, Long Island range during an early international match.

The firing line at Creedmoor during international matches sponsored by the National Rifle Association as portrayed by A. B. Frost.

Gun Digest *editor John Amber takes aim with an early heavy barrel caplock match rifle. Note the bullet starter, false muzzle and powder funnel on the bench in front of him.*

special attention to this part of their business. Not only was their machinery employed to make some of the finest American arms, but in 1873 the German government ordered a complete set of the Pratt & Whitney milling machines, cold pressing and stamping machines, drilling or chucking machines (with horizontal revolving head), tapping machines, four-spindle drills, broaching presses, marking machines, screw machines and rifling machines.

This advanced gunmaking machinery permitted close tolerances to be held and, of course, controlled the uniformity and inter-changeability of parts, the goal sought years earlier in the Eli Whitney factory. As good as was this machinery, however, it still took skilled hands to guide it.

CHAPTER TWENTY-FIVE

Shooting Becomes Scientific

We have had a chance to consider the aesthetic fascination and historical interest of the handmade Kentucky rifles and a wide variety of martial arms earlier in this narrative; a close look at the precision-made "single shots" now is in order. There was a number of factors that contributed to the popularity of the American single shot rifles. Among them was the increasing interest in match shooting following the International Matches at Creedmoor. Establishment of the Walnut Hill range in 1876 by the Massachusetts Rifle Association gave a great boost to shooting at the shorter ranges. The North

Unconventional posture was not uncommon among the early match shooters. This gentleman is using a Remington rolling block.

American Schuetzen Bund had been organized as early as 1865 and clubs had spread to almost every community where there were citizens of Swiss or Teutonic ancestry.

Other factors contributing to the increasing interest in match shooting were the various scientific studies of ballistics, rifling, sights, and actions. All these areas played a part in establishing target accuracy. Among those whose studies and contributions are well known is Dr. Franklin W. Mann, author of *The Bullet's Flight from Powder to Target*. Another early researcher who developed an advanced system of rifling was George Schalck of Pottsville,

Pennsylvania. Many skilled persons contributed to making the beautiful, precise instrument the single shot rifle became.

Remington and Sharps were, of course, the pioneers in the field and Remington's rolling-block and Sharps' sidehammer rifles were very popular. Both manufacturers, however, soon turned to newer models. L. L. Hepburn of Remington developed a dropping-block model known as the Remington-Hepburn. Like the rolling block, it too had a thumb lever to open the breech. A limited number of rifles were improved by a long-time Remington employee, L. N. Walker, who redesigned the

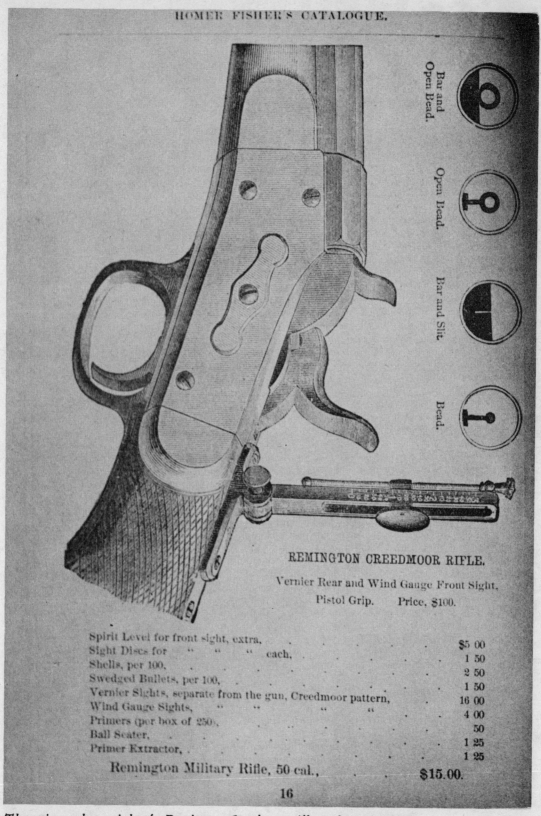

Bar and
Open Bead.

Open Bead.

Bar and Slit.

Bead.

REMINGTON CREEDMOOR RIFLE.

Vernier Rear and Wind Gauge Front Sight,
Pistol Grip.   Price, $100.

Spirit Level for front sight, extra,	$5 00
Sight Discs for " " " each,	1 50
Shells, per 100,	2 50
Swedged Bullets, per 100,	1 50
Vernier Sights, separate from the gun, Creedmoor pattern,	16 00
Wind Gauge Sights, " " " "	4 00
Primers (per box of 250),	50
Ball Seater,	1 25
Primer Extractor,	1 25

Remington Military Rifle, 50 cal., $15.00.

16

The action and rear sight of a Remington Creedmoor rifle as shown in Homer
Fisher's Score Book and Catalogue, published in New York in 1876.

Remington single shot rifles came in a variety of models. From top: Engraved target model with Rigby type barrel, caliber 22 No. 7, light cadet musket, Hepburn long range target rifle, Hepburn sporting rifle, and Hepburn heavy barrel match or buffalo rifle.

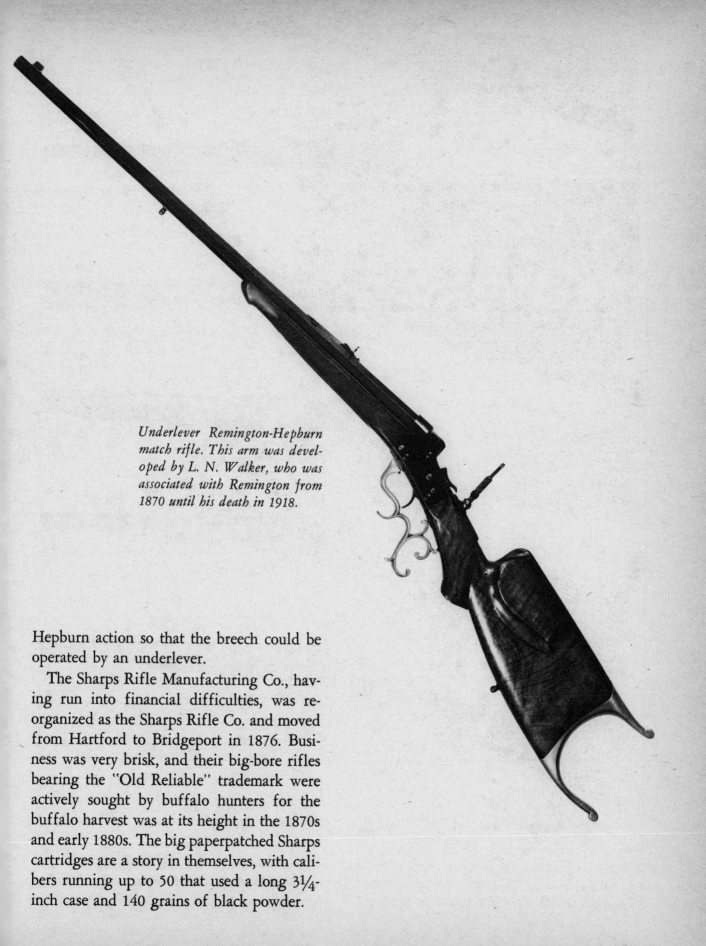

Underlever Remington-Hepburn match rifle. This arm was developed by L. N. Walker, who was associated with Remington from 1870 until his death in 1918.

Hepburn action so that the breech could be operated by an underlever.

The Sharps Rifle Manufacturing Co., having run into financial difficulties, was reorganized as the Sharps Rifle Co. and moved from Hartford to Bridgeport in 1876. Business was very brisk, and their big-bore rifles bearing the "Old Reliable" trademark were actively sought by buffalo hunters for the buffalo harvest was at its height in the 1870s and early 1880s. The big paperpatched Sharps cartridges are a story in themselves, with calibers running up to 50 that used a long 3¼-inch case and 140 grains of black powder.

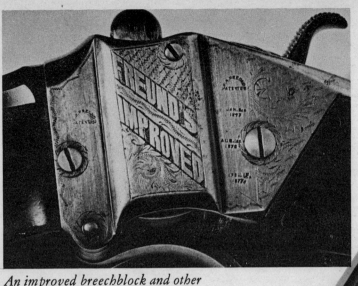

An improved breechblock and other alterations were applied to Sharps rifles by Frank Freund in the 1870s. From the Ralph A. Millermaster collection.

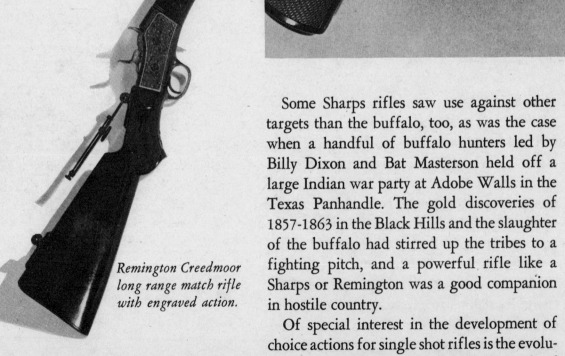

Another of Freund's excellent carbines, made by Freund on the basic Sharps principle in Cheyenne, Wyoming Territory.

Remington Creedmoor long range match rifle with engraved action.

Some Sharps rifles saw use against other targets than the buffalo, too, as was the case when a handful of buffalo hunters led by Billy Dixon and Bat Masterson held off a large Indian war party at Adobe Walls in the Texas Panhandle. The gold discoveries of 1857-1863 in the Black Hills and the slaughter of the buffalo had stirred up the tribes to a fighting pitch, and a powerful rifle like a Sharps or Remington was a good companion in hostile country.

Of special interest in the development of choice actions for single shot rifles is the evolution of the Sharps. Frank W. Freund of

A pair of superb Sharps top grade rifles, an engraved sidehammer mid-range model (above) and an elegant Borchardt model.

Cheyenne, Wyoming, introduced his improvements to the Sharps sidehammer action, and this trend was continued at the Bridgeport factory in developing the 1877 sidehammer model. The breechblock and lock were smaller, the hammer more refined and all-in-all the result was a very handsome (and expensive) gun. The day of the 1877 sidehammer model was short, however, for in 1878 a new action — the streamlined, concealed-hammer Borchardt model—was introduced by the Sharps company. This proved to be one of the finest single shot actions ever made. It became a favorite of A. O. Zischang, one of the great custom riflemakers, who set up shop at Syracuse, New York, in 1879. Zischang and famed barrelmaker Harry Pope assisted Dr. Mann in many of his ballistic experiments. The great marksman Dr. W. G. Hudson used a Zischang barreled rifle with a Borchardt action.

CHAPTER TWENTY-SIX
More Single Shot Rifles

While Remington and Sharps were busy with their single shot rifle design and production, many other manufacturers were not idle. The ingenious dentist, Dr. Edward Maynard, inventor of the Maynard tape primer, had contracted with the Massachusetts Arms Co. of Chicopee Falls, Massachusetts, to produce a rifle of his invention with a tip-up barrel. Proceeding through a variety of cartridge designs, the Maynard rifle in models 1873 and 1882 became a desirable target rifle. One of the drawbacks was that the 1873 rifles at first were chambered for an odd assortment of unique Maynard calibers and cartridges; later, cartridges of a more standard nature were adopted. Models ranged from a 22 to a 44-100 "Long Range Creedmoor Rifle." This Maynard system provided great ease in interchanging barrels, and was highly recommended by A. C. Gould, a prominent contemporary editor and gun book author. There were inadequacies in the Maynard, however, and despite its excellent workmanship the popular trend veered away to other and stronger actions.

The J. Stevens Arms & Tool Co., also of Chicopee Falls, acquired the Massachusetts Arms Co. assets and manufacturing rights and ended 30 years of Maynard production. They were content to bury the Maynard system for they had an excellent product of their own.

Joshua Stevens had started his gunmaking shop in 1864, producing single shot pistols. His Lord, Gould and Conlin target-type pistol models in small caliber became very popular. The business was incorporated in 1886 and not many years later, the Stevens "Ideal" rifles began competing with the finest single shot rifles in the field. One of the greatest barrel-makers of all time, Harry M. Pope, briefly associated with the company and Stevens-Pope match rifles were eagerly sought.

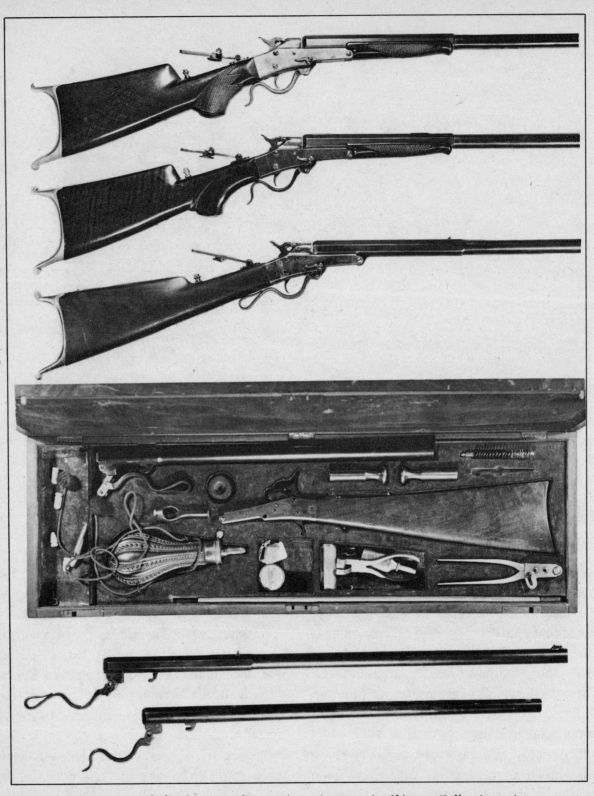

Maynard rifles were made by the Massachusetts Arms Company in Chicopee Falls. At top is a Model 1882, while the others are 1873 models. The cased gun is accompanied by loading tools and interchangeable barrels.

The Stevens Company, organized in 1864, began operations in these modest quarters in Chicopee Falls. Stevens soon became one of the leading manufacturers of quality rifles.

In the "Ideal" line were models from modest Armory models to deluxe engraved and handsomely stocked "Schuetzen" target models. Among the centerfire calibers offered were the 22-15-60 Stevens, the 25-20, 25-21, 25-25, 28-30-120, 32 Ideal, 32-40 and 38-55. These final two calibers were by far the most popular with shooters of that day, regardless of the make of rifle.

The first Stevens action popularly employed was known as the No. 44, but it was soon superseded by the stronger No. 44½, with many of the rifles produced thereafter built on that same general principle. An illustrious

name eventually passed from view when the Stevens company was absorbed by the Savage Arms Co.

Another New England name with a fine reputation and a long history is that of Ballard. Starting in 1861, arms of the Ballard system were made in Worcester, Massachusetts by Ball & Williams; some were made in 1866 by the Merrimack Arms & Mfg. Co. and in 1869 by the Brown Mfg. Co., both of Newburyport, Massachusetts. It was not until the late 1870s and 1880s that the Ballard came into its own as a leading sporting and target rifle. This recognition followed the acquisition of manu-

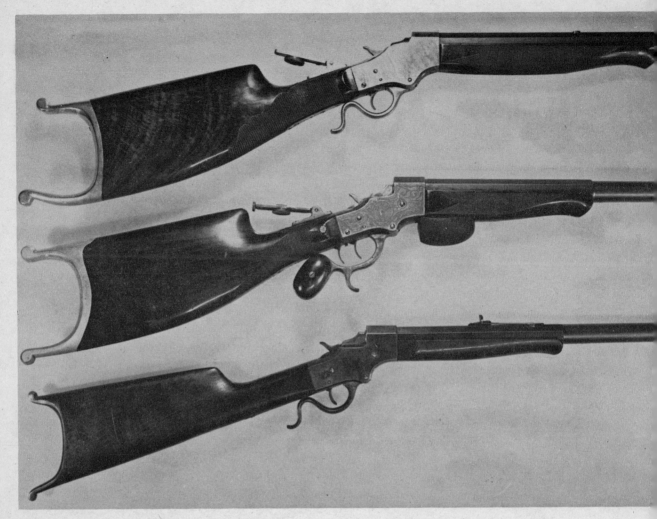

Three Stevens "Ideal" rifles. From top: Target model employing the strong No. 44½ case-hardened frame, a deluxe engraved target model with a No. 44 frame, and a No. 45 Range model with modified buttplate.

facturing rights to the Ballard by John Mahlon Marlin in 1875.

Marlin set to work immediately to improve the basic Ballard action which, despite a somewhat unimpressive history in the hands of the three previous manufacturing firms, represented an excellent, uncomplicated system. When Marlin took over and carefully assembled his improved actions with glass-hard precise component parts of the best metal available, the result was a great foundation for a top quality rifle.

Harry Pope's connection with the Stevens company was terminated in 1905 and there-

A group of early Ballard rifle models. Some had a special breechblock which permitted them to be used with either a metallic cartridge or with percussion caps, loose powder and balls.

A serious marksman who favors the traditional single-shot guns demonstrates the offhand position using a palm rest.

after he operated his own shop. He was one of the premier barrelmakers of the country, along with George C. Schoyen, H. D. Zischang, and Axel Peterson of Denver. All of these great craftsmen built beautiful rifles on the improved Marlin-Ballard action.

While the basic actions now came from New England arms plants, some of the finest match rifles were being barreled, stocked and finished by custom gunmakers in other states —New Jersey, Colorado and Michigan for example, where Pope, Schoyen and Peterson, and Niedner worked.

Match shooting had become a very popular

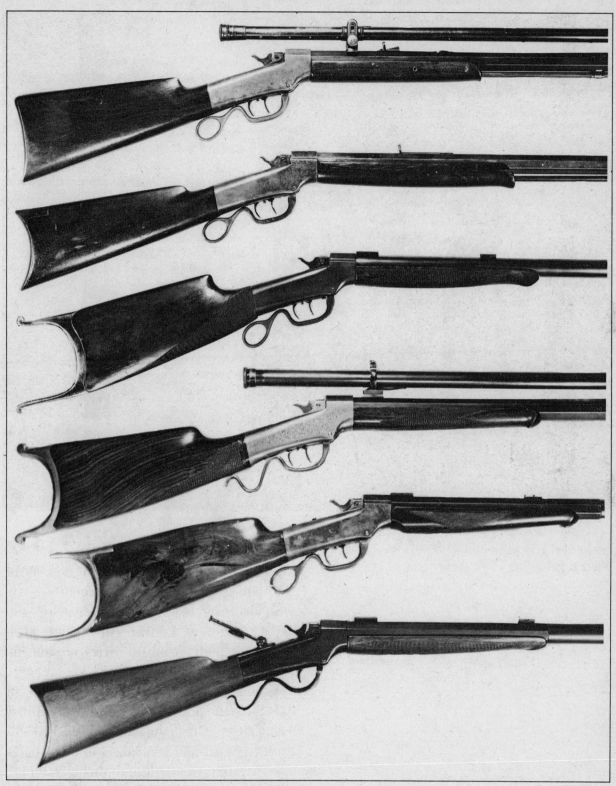

A group of Marlin-Ballard rifles. From top: two Pacific models with rod under barrel, a target model barreled by George C. Schoyen, an engraved target model with Sidle scope, another target rifle barreled by Schoyen, and a target rifle with Stevens-Pope barrel.

Everlasting Center-Fire Shells.

The advantages of the Everlasting Shells are numerous. There is less recoil than with a bottle-neck shell; it is no trouble to clean them; they are exactly the same size as the bore, so that the ball lies in the grooves as in a muzzle loader. The rifle can be used as a muzzle loader, one shell answering for hundreds of shots, with the advantage of being able to see the condition of the barrel if desired, and having the cap covered, preventing blowing back, the cap and powder being in close contact. They are made of heavy metal, specially prepared, and a fine quality of powder can be used, which would burst an ordinary shell and endanger the life of the shooter. There is no bother about reducing after discharging. They are cheaper in the long run than ordinary shells, as each one will last for years, if properly used and thoroughly cleaned after firing, so that they do not corrode.

Everlasting shells as used in the early Marlin-Ballard models.

32-40 GR'S	38-55 GR'S	40-63 GR'S	40-85 GR'S	45-70 GR'S	45-100 GR'S
5 cts. each.	6 cts. each.	7 cts. each.	8 cts. each.	7 cts. each.	10 cts. each.

Everlasting Shells of all sizes take the No. 2½ Primer.

A variety of bullets were offered for use in the Marlin-Ballards.

MARLIN FIRE ARMS CO., NEW HAVEN, CONN.

BULLETS.
PATCHED.

32-165	32-185	38-255	38-330	40-285	40-330	40
$10.00	$9.75	$11.00	$11.50	$11.00	$11.50	$

PRICE PER 1,000.

GROOVED.

32-185	38-255	38-330	40-260	40-285	40-330	45-285	45
$7.75	$9.50	$11.00	$9.00	$9.50	$11.00	$9.50	$

PRICE PER 1,000.

Other Bullets.

32 Calibre,	165 Grains,	Grooved,	per 1000,	
44 "	405 "	Patched,	"	
45 "	420 "	"	"	
45 "	550 "	"	"	

164

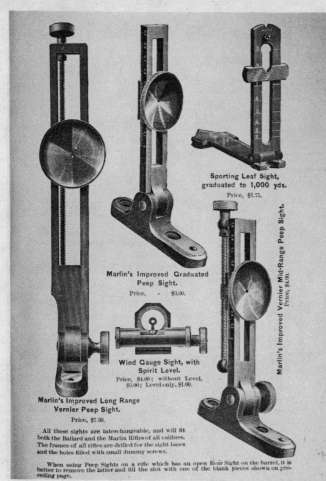

Sporting Leaf Sight,
graduated to 1,000 yds.
Price, $1.75.

Marlin's Improved Graduated
Peep Sight.
Price, - $3.00.

Marlin's Improved Vernier Mid-Range Peep Sight.
Price, $4.00.

Wind Gauge Sight, with
Spirit Level.
Price, $4.00 ; without Level,
$3.00; Level only, $1.00.

Marlin's Improved Long Range
Vernier Peep Sight.
Price, $7.50.

All these sights are interchangeable, and will fit
both the Ballard and the Marlin Rifles of all calibres.
The frames of all rifles are drilled for the sight bases
and the holes filled with small dummy screws.

When using Peep Sights on a rifle which has an open Rear Sight on the barrel, it is
better to remove the latter and fill the slot with one of the blank pieces shown on pre-
ceding page.

*Quality sights were a must
for the serious match
shooter. These were
offered by Marlin for use
on their Ballard rifles.*

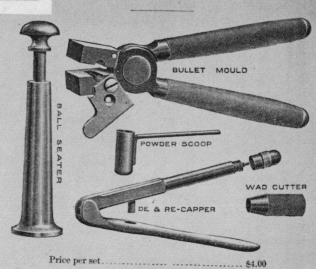

MARLIN FIRE ARMS CO., NEW HAVEN, CONN.

LARD RE-LOADING TOOLS.

BULLET MOULD

BALL SEATER

POWDER SCOOP

WAD CUTTER

DE & RE-CAPPER

*The Everlasting shells
could be reloaded many
times, and Marlin offered
the tools with which to
load them.*

Price per set.. $4.00

The above cut shows a complete set of Tools for Ballard Rifle, consisting
of 5 separate pieces.

They can be furnished in 32-40, 38-55, 40-63, 40-85, and 45-100, which
are the present sizes in use, also in 38-50, 40-65, and 40-90, which were
formerly made.

The Ball Seater simply *seats* the ball in the shell, and does not crimp the
latter. This is preferable in target shooting and the only feasible plan when
patched bullets are used. If it is desired to crimp the cartridges, the Ideal
Reloading Tools should be used.

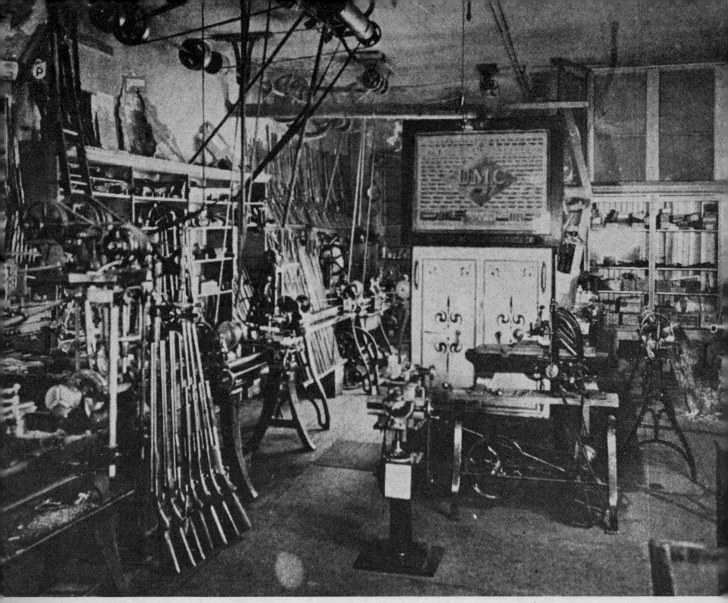

The 19th century gunmaker's shop was a crowded place. This is Axel Peterson's shop in Denver.

sport in Colorado, where experts like C. W. Rowland had shot a perfect machine rest score of 10 shots at 200 yards with a Peterson 32-40 barrel. D. W. King of the Colorado Rifle Club had established a new world record in 1904 by recording a score of 917 offhand on the Standing American Target, surpassing Pope's long-standing record score of 908. King's rifle was equipped with a barrel made by George Schoyen of Denver.

CHAPTER TWENTY-SEVEN
John Browning's First Rifle

In Utah, just west of Colorado, a young mechanical genius named John M. Browning had his own ideas about rifles. From his workbench eventually came the single shot action he patented in 1879. Browning's action had some major points of novelty, but did not involve a new principle. The morticed breechblock was lowered by action of a lever, very similar to the system used by the Sharps which had been patented back in 1848. But Browning's design had important refinements such as a centrally hung hammer, a strong streamlined frame and a much improved lock mechanism.

John M. Browning's 1878 single shot rifle (top) and the improved Model 1879 which he patented below it. A few were made by Browning Brothers in Ogden, Utah, before Browning granted the manufacturing license to Winchester. This design became the Winchester "High Wall" and "Low Wall" actions.

It was to be a practice followed by Browning during his early life that he was more interested in inventing and improving arms systems than in manufacturing them. As a result, in 1883 the Browning rights to manufacture guns of his 1879 design were transferred to Winchester, resulting in production of Winchester's famous "High Wall" and "Low Wall" single shot rifles which they first classified as the Model of 1885. Another fine single shot rifle was thus added to the others produced along the Connecticut valley.

The High Wall model, so named because of its high-sided hammer channel and basic strength, came into popular use by some of the best custom riflemakers, including Harry Pope. The 1886 Winchester catalog revealed that the single shot rifle was made in 28 centerfire and 10 rimfire calibers. As manufacture developed, many models were offered from plain plinking or hunting rifles to deluxe "Schuetzen" models.

One of the popular Winchester small bore single shot rifles was a 22 rimfire called a *Winder Musket* in honor of Colonel Charles B. Winder, a great marksman who was credited with contributions to the design. These 22 rifles, some using High Wall and

Winchester variations of the basic Browning design. From top: High Wall sporting model, Winder armory 22 musket, Low Wall sporting model, deluxe Low Wall with special high breechblock, Low Wall 410 shotgun, and deluxe engraved Low Wall with pistol grip.

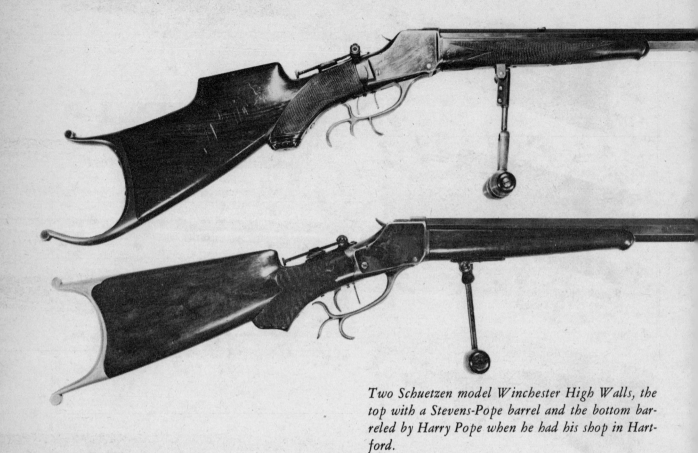

Two Schuetzen model Winchester High Walls, the top with a Stevens-Pope barrel and the bottom barreled by Harry Pope when he had his shop in Hartford.

some Low Wall actions, were called Armory Models, and became official rifles for indoor training and match competition. At one time the Winder musket could be obtained by members of the NRA through the Director of Civilian Marksmanship (War Department) for $18.80. The Stevens armory musket of similar fullstock type was priced at $15.

There were many other good single shot rifles made in this period, among which were the Frank Wesson, Wurfflein, Slotterbek, Peabody-Martini, and Phoenix, but few gained great recognition.

It should be noted that some of the stronger single shot actions have been used to build rifles chambered for the so-called "wildcat" loads — non-factory cartridge case designs meant to achieve higher velocities and give exceptional accuracy.

For true quality in gunmaking, the better grades of the single shot match rifles have few superiors. The books on this subject by such long-time students of the subject as James J. Grant and Frank de Haas are interesting and very informative. Another devotee of this kind of rifle, John T. Amber, has contributed much through his own writings and the publishing vehicles he directs.

An interesting group of single shot rifles. From top: Marlin-Ballard "Union Hill" target, Marlin-Ballard Rigby offhand model, Foel rifle made by Deringer in Philadelphia, Cyphers rifle made in Greenville, Michigan, and Charles Slotterbek rifle made in Lakeport, California.

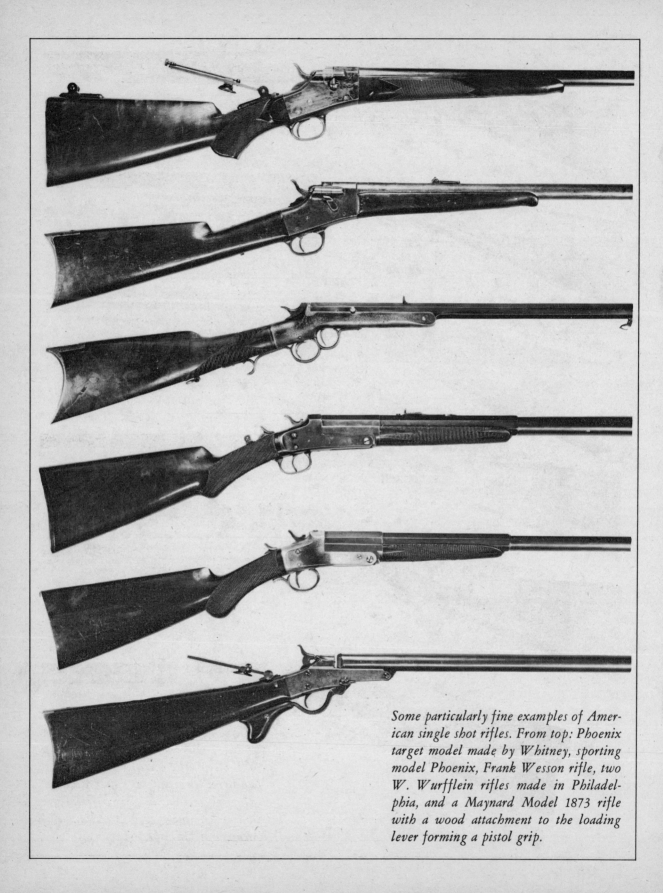

Some particularly fine examples of American single shot rifles. From top: Phoenix target model made by Whitney, sporting model Phoenix, Frank Wesson rifle, two W. Wurfflein rifles made in Philadelphia, and a Maynard Model 1873 rifle with a wood attachment to the loading lever forming a pistol grip.

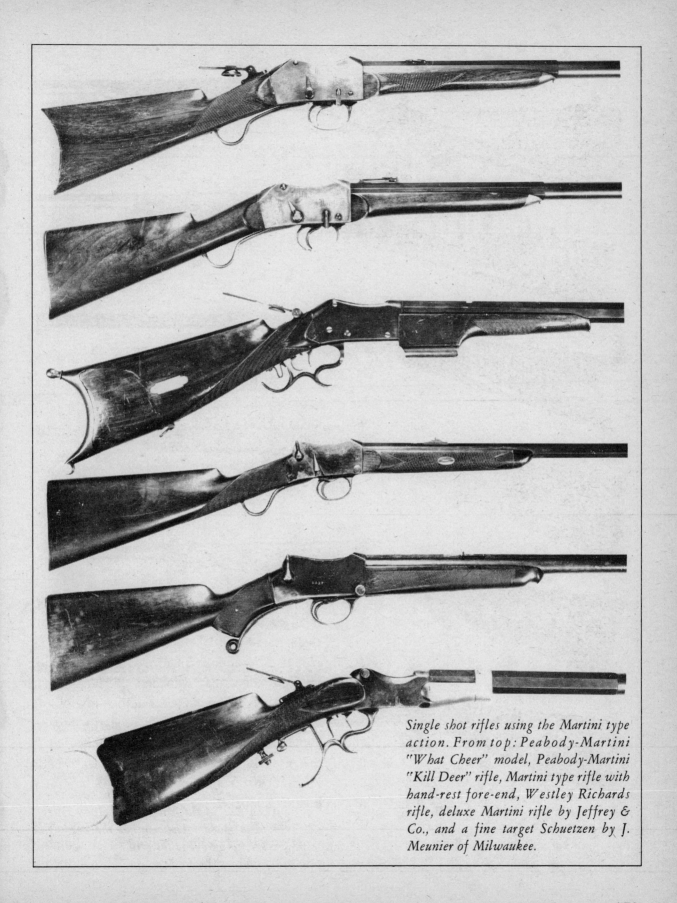

Single shot rifles using the Martini type action. From top: Peabody-Martini "What Cheer" model, Peabody-Martini "Kill Deer" rifle, Martini type rifle with hand-rest fore-end, Westley Richards rifle, deluxe Martini rifle by Jeffrey & Co., and a fine target Schuetzen by J. Meunier of Milwaukee.

CHAPTER TWENTY-EIGHT

Repeating Rifles Come Into Their Own

Although great interest was shown (and still continues today) in the finer single shot rifles, the lesser guns of this type were gradually pushed from the picture by repeating arms. Winchester, Marlin, Savage, Bullard, Burgess, Colt, and a few others all introduced lever-action repeating rifles. Some trombone or slide action repeaters such as Colt's "Lightning" model and Winchester's Model 1890 (another Browning invention) became available.

As the end of the 19th century approached, armsmaking evolution had led to the bolt action guns such as the Hotchkiss, Ward-Burton,

Berdan, Lee and Chaffee-Reece. Box magazine repeaters such as the Lee straight-pull bolt action rifle and the lever-action 1895 Winchester appeared. Ventures were begun to compete with the dominant foreign production of shotguns, including lever-action and trombone repeaters. Smokeless powder was introduced in 1896 for the new bolt action Krag magazine rifles adopted by the Army. Semi-automatic rifles and pistols were just around the corner.

The Spanish-American War of 1898 was of short duration and had very conclusive results. After the battleship Maine had been blown up while on a good-will tour to Cuba, the U.S. Navy responded with a vengeance, destroying the Spanish fleet. The Marines landed at Guantanamo Bay. Major General Shafter landed 10,000 men, including the 1st U.S. Volunteer Cavalry which had been recruited by Lieutenant Colonel Theodore Roosevelt. A decisive victory was won at San Juan Hill. The end result was the elimination of Spain from all the lands discovered by Columbus. The U.S. acquired Puerto Rico, Guam and the Philippines in addition to guaranteeing Cuban independence.

Some of the U.S. forces still were armed

A variety of American lever action rifles were marketed during the late 1800s. From top: two Burgess patent Whitneyvilles in 45-70 and 44-40 calibers, Evans 44 caliber sporting model from Maine, Marlin Model 1895 take-down in 45-70, top grade Marlin Model 1894 in 38-40, and Marlin Model 1881 top ejection in 45-70.

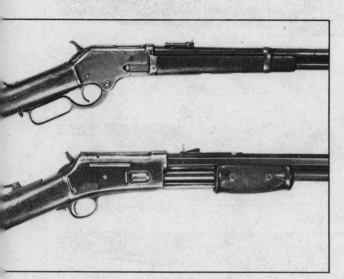

Colt, traditionally a handgun manufacturer, entered the rifle market in the 1880s with both lever action and slide action models.

Some uncommon American repeating rifles. From top: Deluxe engraved 40 caliber Marlin, 50 caliber Bullard, Standard 35 caliber convertible (semi-automatic or pump action), Lee straight-pull sporter caliber 236, and Blake 30-40 rotary magazine model.

with the trusty 45-70 trapdoor Springfields during these hostilities, but Teddy Roosevelt would have none of these for his men, who were issued the new Krag magazine rifles. The Krag had its baptism of fire in Cuba and performed well. It proved to be a very reliable gun, with a nice, smooth action, the first of the official 30 caliber U.S. military rifles. When they were superseded by the Springfield 1903 many Krag rifles finally found their way into the hands of civilians and were re-worked into fine sporters for hunting.

The necked 30-40 rimmed cartridge used in the Krag was—and is—quite effective for

A rifle team of the New Jersey National Guard pictured with their Krag-Jorgensen 30-40 carbines, in 1903.

most American game. When the change-over was made to the stronger Springfield action, with two locking lugs instead of the one of the Krag, more powerful 30-03 and 30-06 rimless necked cartridges were designed. The cartridge remains very popular to the present.

New capacity for government production of U.S. arms was added with the improvement of the facilities at the Rock Island Arsenal. Military production would be quite stable in the first decade of the 1900s, attention centering on the Springfield rifle. For side arms, the double-action Army and Navy Colt 38 and the 45 Colt double-action revolvers (with

bird-head grip) sufficed until the New Service 45 came along in 1909. Smith & Wesson's first major military contribution had been their single-action Schofield 45 top-break model, and a solid frame "New Century" model in 1908.

In the civilian rifle field, Winchester lever-action models from 1873 had evolved through the '78, '86, '92, '94 and '95, several of these showing John Browning's inventive genius. But plenty of competition was developing for Winchester as the new century proceeded. One of the most formidable in the lever-action field was Savage's 1899 repeating rifle, a ba-

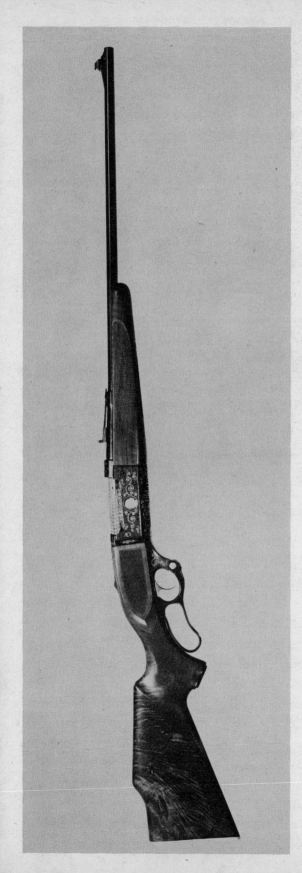

Savage's Model 99 has long been one of the American shooter's most popular arms. The example, serial number 1,000,000, was presented to the National Rifle Association for their museum in 1960.

sically excellent hammerless model, which like the 30-30 caliber 1894 Winchester has continued in popularity, with some modifications, to the present. Remington and Marlin kept pace, improving and updating their competitive models.

Early bolt action carbines. From top: Winchester-made Hotchkiss model 1879, Berdan circa 1868, and Lee Model 1879 made by Remington.

Colt's revolver line since the early 20th century has consisted primarily of swing-out cylinder double-action models. Note the Camp Perry Model at upper left, a single-shot on a revolver frame, and the two special-order pocket pistols at upper right factory modified by John Fitzgerald.

CHAPTER TWENTY-NINE

America's First Automatics

One of the major developments of the new century was in the area of semi-automatic arms. Europe had gotten the jump on us in this field, with the Borchardt, Mannlicher, Bergmann, Mauser and many others. Close behind, however, was the genius of John Browning and the development by Colt of his principles in self-loading, semi-automatic pistols. Colt-made pistols on Browning's patents made their appearance at the start of the 20th century, just about the same time as the Luger pistol, developed from the original Borchardt, made its appearance. Both were destined to long service.

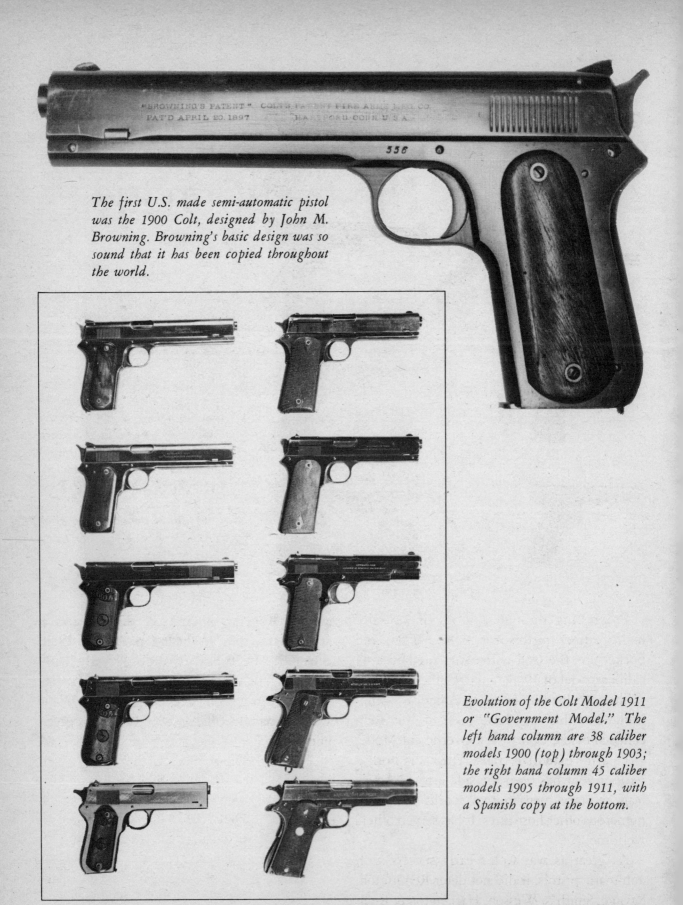

The first U.S. made semi-automatic pistol was the 1900 Colt, designed by John M. Browning. Browning's basic design was so sound that it has been copied throughout the world.

Evolution of the Colt Model 1911 or "Government Model." The left hand column are 38 caliber models 1900 (top) through 1903; the right hand column 45 caliber models 1905 through 1911, with a Spanish copy at the bottom.

Although Colt has been the most prolific semi-auto pistol maker in the United States, it has had many competitors. Included here are examples from Savage, Remington, Harrington & Richardson, Ruger, High Standard and Reising. Of particular interest is the 45 Savage in the upper left hand corner; one of about 200 made for U.S. Army test in 1906.

Progressing through a series of 38 automatic caliber pistols for Army, Navy and pocket use, the Colt automatics reached a 45 caliber model of 1905, said to be the first large caliber self-loading pistol in America. As important as this may have been, it was soon eclipsed by the Colt U. S. Government Model 1911 after extensive trials. Thus was born a weapon that has been the side arm of American military men in two world wars and numerous other hostilities. It has served others well, too.

As great as was Colt's early success with automatic pistols, it did not deter Remington, Savage, Smith & Wesson, Harrington & Rich- ardson, Ruger, Hi-Standard, Reising and a few others from producing models of their own. The field has expanded greatly with the years to include semi-automatic match target pistols; compact pocket models by various manufacturers now also show great popularity.

CHAPTER THIRTY

American Guns
Go to War in Europe

eturning to the 1911 period, the search for an efficient 45 military pistol was not without serious purpose. War clouds again were hovering on the horizon. World War I soon exploded with all its destruction and misery. War always sparks an energetic scramble to build and equip a civilian army. It is the practice invariably pursued during wartime that production of civilian type arms is stopped and all efforts turned to manufacturing military models. In the case of Colt's Model 1911 military automatic, the demand was so great that contract allocations were made for their manufacture with the

Remington Arms Co., and seven others including the North American Arms Co. Ltd. of Quebec, Canada. As the war in Europe expanded, the allies sent buying commissions to the United States to place orders for thousands of arms. Remington's rifle and ammunition plants in Ilion and Bridgeport were greatly expanded to meet these demands, as were the plants of other major manufacturers.

When the United States entered the war in 1917, there were not enough of the Model '03 Springfield bolt rifles to arm newly raised troops. It was believed that production in the national armories could not be increased fast enough to supply the urgent demand. Already several private American armsmakers were manufacturing the British Enfield Model 1914 rifles in a 303, a rimmed case caliber, so it was decided that it would be quicker to have them adapt this rifle to the 30-06 rimless cartridge for the U.S. forces than retool for the Springfield. As a result, well over a million Enfield rifles, designated as the Model 1917 Springfield but popularly called "Enfields," were produced at the Winchester, Remington and Eddystone Rifle plants.

The year 1917 saw a development in military revolvers also, in which the big Colt New

Original Colt Model 1911 in a commercial version as indicated by the "C" serial number.

Service and Smith & Wesson's service revolvers were modified to use the standard 45 rimless automatic ammunition by use of a metal half-moon clip adapter holding three cartridges—two of these fully loaded the gun. Over 300,000 of the Model 1917 revolvers were produced between 1917 and the end of 1919, approximately half that total by each manufacturer.

Although a detailed study of machine guns is afield from this narrative, they were a part of the American manufacturing scene and vitally important in wartime. Colt had been the principal manufacturer of the Gatling

Springfield Model 1903, standard U.S. rifle in two world wars.

gun, and some recoil and gas operated machine models from England and France, such as the Vickers and Benet-Mercie, were manufactured by Colt in the World War I period. But major production was devoted to the models developed by that versatile genius John M. Browning, some made by Colt, some by Remington and others.

Up to this time the American experience with rapid-fire guns was limited. The Gatling gun, coming to some attention after the War between the States, was prominent in the success of quelling Canada's Riel Rebellion, and perhaps equally important historically by be-

ing left behind when Custer marched his men to death on the Little Big Horn. The Hotchkiss rapid-fire gun came into national attention by its lethal performance at Wounded Knee, a reversal of Custer's defeat, which wrote an end to further large Indian conflicts.

Colt-made 6-barrel Gatling gun with Accles feed, demonstrated by Gun Digest *editor John Amber.*

CHAPTER THIRTY-ONE
America's Armsmakers in the Between-Wars Years

In the two peacetime decades between the World Wars, there was a return to the design and production of hunting and target models. For a time a productive period favored the arms manufacturers, but then came the financial crash of 1929 and worldwide depression. It hit many industries hard, and national income was practically slashed in half.

Remington Arms-UMC was one of the hardest hit, their tremendous wartime expansion of manufacturing facilities at Ilion and Bridgeport involved great indebtedness. An orderly and beneficial transfer took place,

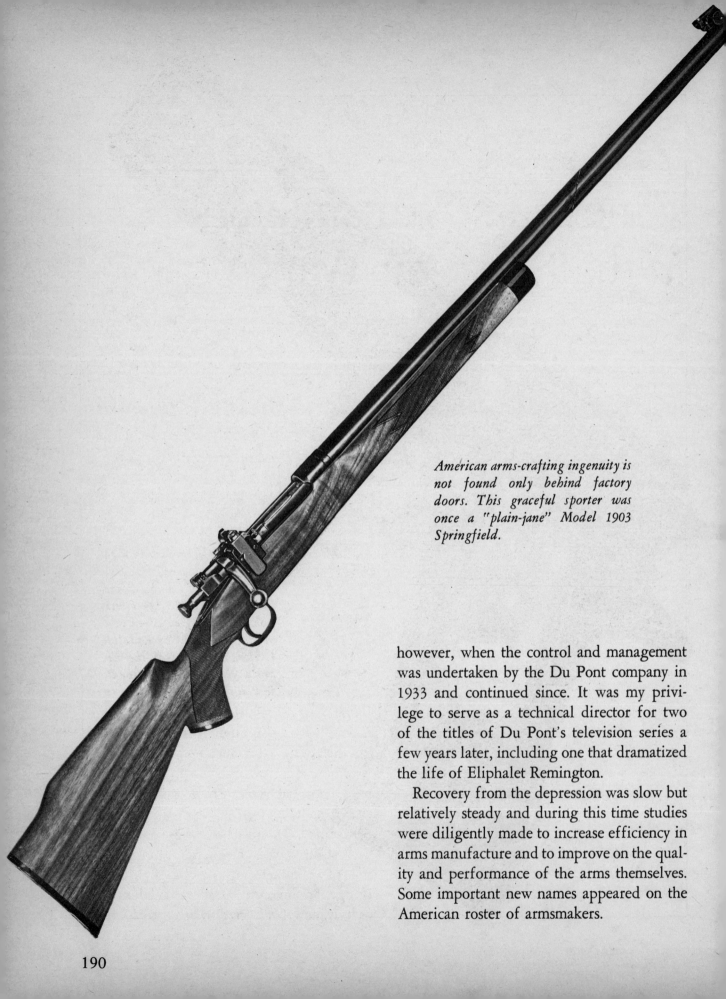

American arms-crafting ingenuity is not found only behind factory doors. This graceful sporter was once a "plain-jane" Model 1903 Springfield.

however, when the control and management was undertaken by the Du Pont company in 1933 and continued since. It was my privilege to serve as a technical director for two of the titles of Du Pont's television series a few years later, including one that dramatized the life of Eliphalet Remington.

Recovery from the depression was slow but relatively steady and during this time studies were diligently made to increase efficiency in arms manufacture and to improve on the quality and performance of the arms themselves. Some important new names appeared on the American roster of armsmakers.

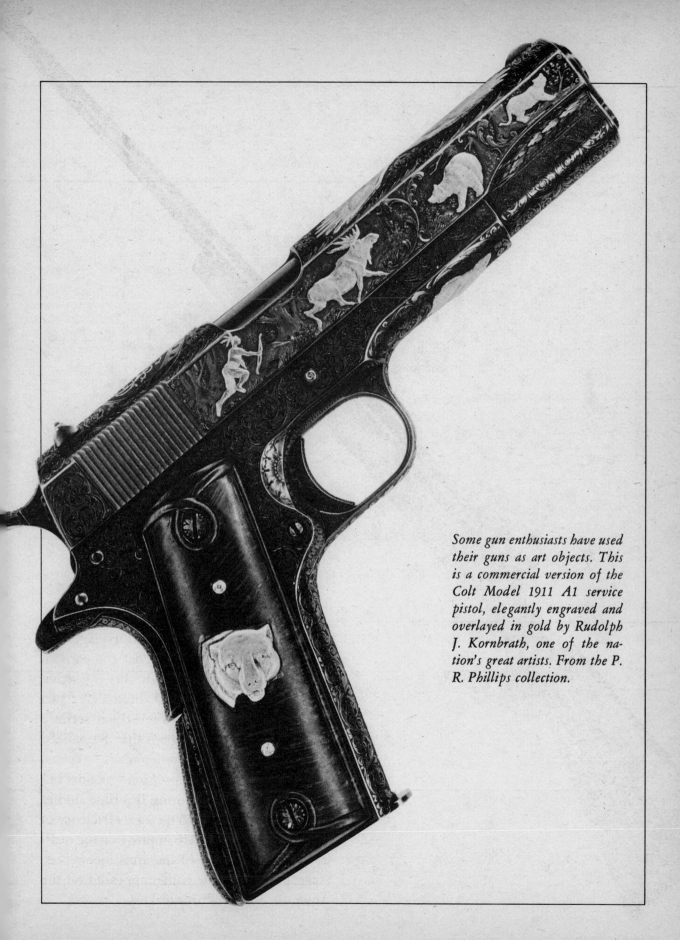

Some gun enthusiasts have used their guns as art objects. This is a commercial version of the Colt Model 1911 A1 service pistol, elegantly engraved and overlayed in gold by Rudolph J. Kornbrath, one of the nation's great artists. From the P. R. Phillips collection.

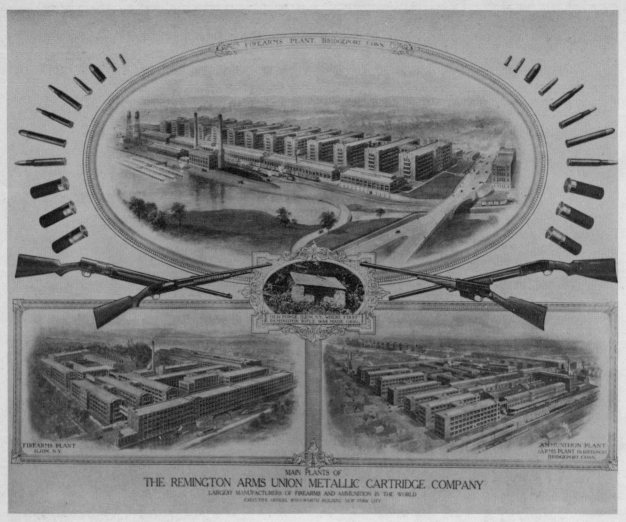

FIREARMS PLANT, BRIDGEPORT, CONN.

OLD FORGE, ILION, N.Y. WHERE FIRST
REMINGTON RIFLE WAS MADE (1816)

FIREARMS PLANT
ILION, N.Y.

AMMUNITION PLANT
(ARMS PLANT IN BOTANCO)
BRIDGEPORT, CONN.

MAIN PLANTS OF
THE REMINGTON ARMS UNION METALLIC CARTRIDGE COMPANY
LARGEST MANUFACTURERS OF FIREARMS AND AMMUNITION IN THE WORLD
EXECUTIVE OFFICES, WOOLWORTH BUILDING, NEW YORK CITY

The American arms-making industry is a big one, and the major manufacturers have quite extensive facilities. This factory broadside shows the Remington Arms—UMC plants at Bridgeport, Connecticut and Ilion, New York as they appeared about 1920.

Autoloading rifles joined the lever-action, slide-action and bolt-action models. Sportsmen and target shooters were provided with a great range of makes and models from which to choose. In addition to the autoloading semi-automatic pistols, revolvers and rifles, the American-made shotgun took on new stature. These, too, were offered in a variety of actions and types including the autoloading, slide action, side-by-side and over/under doubles as well as single barrel guns.

Many new names joined the armsmaker's ranks in the post-World War II days. Rutger, for example, began as a pistolmaker but has since broadened production to include rifles.

A pair of hunters, one with a side-by-side double-barrel shotgun and the other with an over-under, take aim at a flock of canvasbacks.

Colt's Police Positive was a simple, straight-forward compact pistol that was very popular with police, guard services and many others. This example was made in the early 1930s for Railway Express, whose marking appears on the backstrap.

CHAPTER THIRTY-TWO
The Great American Shotgun

Two great names in American-made double-barrel shotguns disappeared when the L.C. Smith company was taken over by Hunter Arms Co. and Parker Brothers was taken over by the Remington Arms Co. I have owned and shot both the L.C. Smith and Parker guns and could not ask for finer firearms. Both companies had been founded before the turn of the century. The hard laws of economics rather than the quality of their product apparently caused their demise. Both Parker and L.C. Smith guns are actively sought by gun buffs today.

Parker Bros. models were continued by

Camouflaged against the snow with a bedsheet, the hunter and his Winchester
Model 12 have managed to outwit a brace of wily crows.

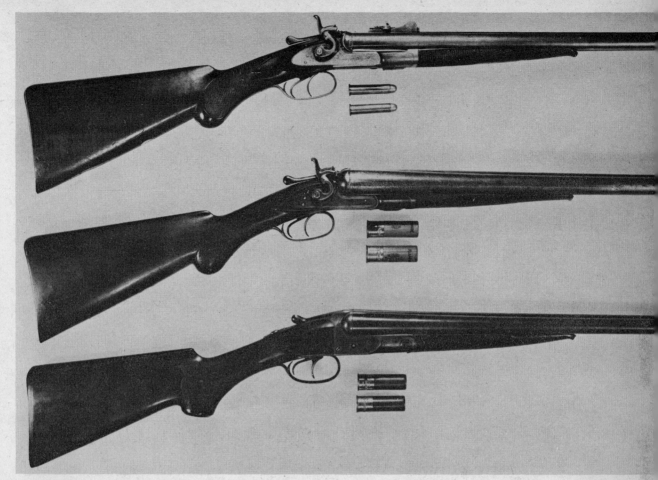

Colt, though traditionally a manufacturer of handguns, also made double-barrel shotguns in the 1880s and 1890s. Both hammer and hammerless versions are shown here, along with a very rare Colt double-barrel rifle (top).

Remington from 1936 to 1940, but after World War II the Remington line was continued with greater emphasis on the repeating shotgun models and the Parker line was abandoned. Winchester's popular Model 12 slide-action repeating shotgun was joined by their most illustrious double-barrel model in 1931, the Model 21, one of the greatest American doubles. This excellent shotgun has been favorably compared to the best English makes such as the Holland & Holland or Purdey. Other manufacturers also noted for quality doubles were Ithaca and Fox (acquired by Savage).

Throughout the history of shotgun manufacture, and especially in the double-barrel models, the barrels themselves gave the most problems. Some manufacturers imported barrels from England, Belgium or other nations. First in order of appearance were the so-called Damascus barrels. These were made of iron and steel "blades," alternated and then welded into a bar, the bar then twisted into a tight spiral rod. One or more rods would be wrapped around a mandrel and welded to form a barrel. The process of twisting and welding gave the finished barrel strength in all directions. The finished barrel was then "pickled" in an acid solution which affected the iron and steel components differently, thus producing a figured pattern.

As attractive as the Damascus barrels might be in appearance, they did lack the strength necessary to withstand the pressures of the more powerful shells being developed. Improvements, such as those of Dan Lefever's hammerless model which eliminated the outside hammers, provided better hinging and locking of the barrels, and incorporated fluid, pressed steel barrels. This, along with introduction of smokeless powder which eliminated the obscuring cloud of black powder smoke from the second shot, finally brought the American doubles to a highly efficient sporting arm—although in the early days doubles were also used for other than sports.

We have seen in this century the rise and fall of the double shotgun in popular usage. Most shotguns sold today are the single-barrel repeating models using autoloading or slide actions. A few purists, however, still favor the doubles. The high price for the top quality double-barrel guns no doubt is a major obstacle to greater popularity, although over-under doubles appear to be having a resurgence of interest. ※

CHAPTER THIRTY-THREE
The Army Adopts the Garand

Turning from sporting fields to the military in the between-the-wars period, the U.S. Ordnance Department kept active in searching for improvements for its weapons arsenal. One important result was the adoption of a self-loading design for U.S. service rifles. John Garand invented the system which was developed at Springfield Armory. This was a clip-fed, gas-operated, self-loading arm which was adopted in 1936 and became known as the "U.S. Rifle, Cal. 30, M1." Winchester was the firm given a contract to manufacture these arms in 1939 and continued to manufacture them through

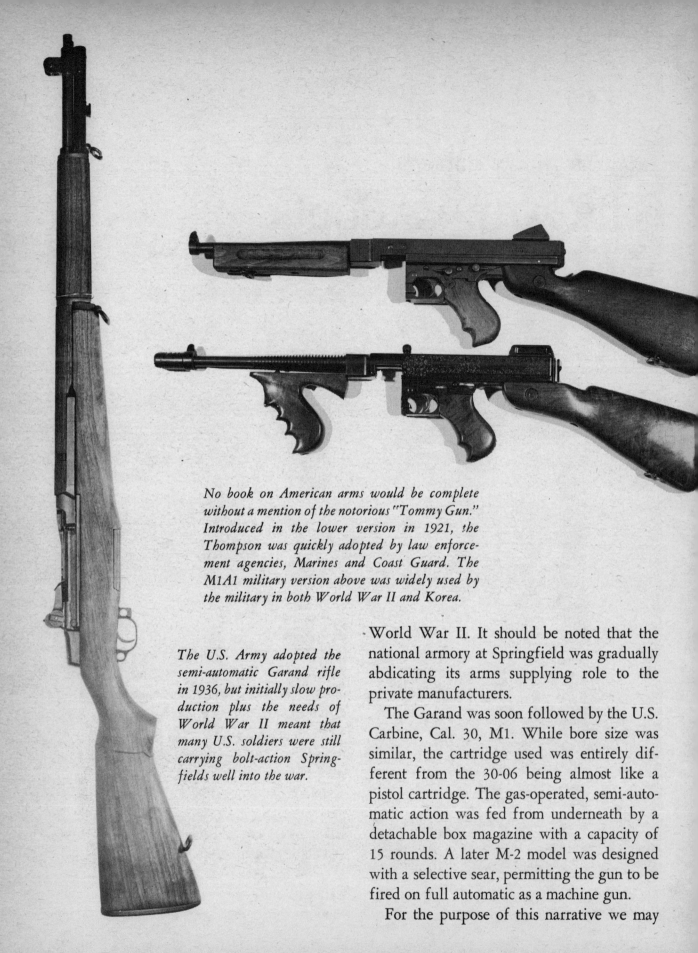

No book on American arms would be complete without a mention of the notorious "Tommy Gun." Introduced in the lower version in 1921, the Thompson was quickly adopted by law enforcement agencies, Marines and Coast Guard. The M1A1 military version above was widely used by the military in both World War II and Korea.

The U.S. Army adopted the semi-automatic Garand rifle in 1936, but initially slow production plus the needs of World War II meant that many U.S. soldiers were still carrying bolt-action Springfields well into the war.

World War II. It should be noted that the national armory at Springfield was gradually abdicating its arms supplying role to the private manufacturers.

The Garand was soon followed by the U.S. Carbine, Cal. 30, M1. While bore size was similar, the cartridge used was entirely different from the 30-06 being almost like a pistol cartridge. The gas-operated, semi-automatic action was fed from underneath by a detachable box magazine with a capacity of 15 rounds. A later M-2 model was designed with a selective sear, permitting the gun to be fired on full automatic as a machine gun.

For the purpose of this narrative we may

Though replaced by first the M14 and later the AR-15 for general use, the M1 Garand still saw service in Viet Nam as a sniper's rifle.

GI ingenuity—this infantryman, on patrol in Viet Nam, has doubled his M14's firepower by taping two magazines together. Photograph courtesy U.S. Army.

The M14 was a modernized version of the Garand, somewhat lighter and with an increased capacity removable magazine.

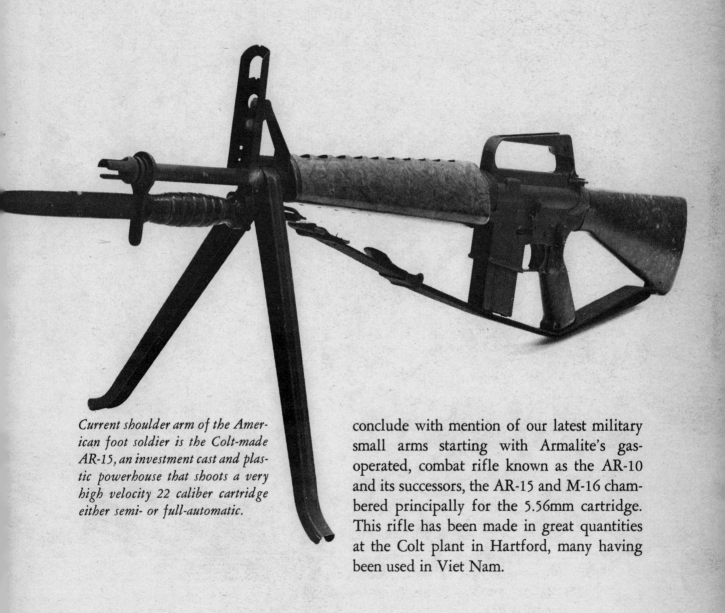

Current shoulder arm of the American foot soldier is the Colt-made AR-15, an investment cast and plastic powerhouse that shoots a very high velocity 22 caliber cartridge either semi- or full-automatic.

conclude with mention of our latest military small arms starting with Armalite's gas-operated, combat rifle known as the AR-10 and its successors, the AR-15 and M-16 chambered principally for the 5.56mm cartridge. This rifle has been made in great quantities at the Colt plant in Hartford, many having been used in Viet Nam.

A watchful GI with his AR-15 at the ready in a Viet Nam rice paddy.

CHAPTER THIRTY-FOUR

The Postwar American Arms Industry

Much has transpired in arms design and manufacturing practices and particularly in the corporate composition of arms manufacturers in the years following World War II.

A growth in holding companies or "conglomerates," as some are called, has greatly affected the ownership and management of the nation's major armsmakers. In effect, this represents formation of a large corporation with greatly diversified divisions of which armsmaking may be but one.

This trend has not appeared to lessen productivity or efficiency but in fact may have

Ruger is a relative newcomer in the field of high grade bolt action and autoloading sporting rifles.

increased it. We find the relatively newer armsmakers like Weatherby, Hi-Standard and Sturm, Ruger & Co. offering a range of models in active competition with the plants whose continual services in gunmaking go back a century or more. Manufacturers who once made only pistols and revolvers now offer a full line including rifles and shotguns. Not only are there more major manufacturers, but the range of models many offer now encompasses the whole field of firearms. There has been a comparable proliferation, too, in the field of gun accessory manufacturers. A look through any of the major gun magazines

A lot of water has flowed down the Connecticut river and many new models introduced since the first guns were shipped from the plants now producing these bolt action rifles. From left: Winchester, Smith & Wesson and Colt.

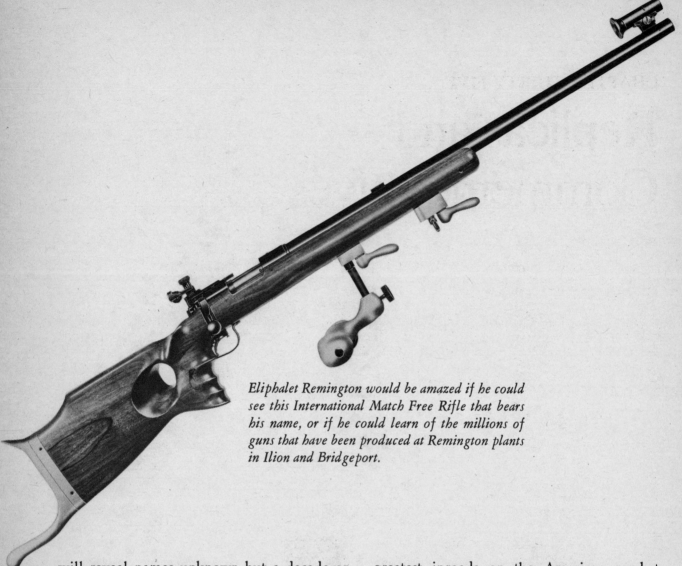

Eliphalet Remington would be amazed if he could see this International Match Free Rifle that bears his name, or if he could learn of the millions of guns that have been produced at Remington plants in Ilion and Bridgeport.

will reveal names unknown but a decade or less ago.

One of the practices which has met mixed public reaction is the importation and sale of foreign-made gun models by traditional American manufacturers. It is a practice not limited to arms manufacturers. Major American automobile manufacturers merchandise foreign-made models, especially in the compact car field. The electronics field is another area in which this practice is widespread. In arms, the foreign shotguns, bolt-action sporting rifles, automatic pistols and the less expensive revolvers seem to have made the

greatest inroads on the American market, many of them bearing the names of and sold by some of our best known firms.

CHAPTER THIRTY-FIVE

Replicas and Commemoratives

s to importations, a relatively new field has been the development of replica arms. At first, enterprising arms dealers had working replicas of famous American antique pistol and rifle models produced in Belgium, Italy, Spain, and other foreign countries where cheaper manufacturing costs prevailed. It was not long, however, before American manufacturers like Colt, Ruger, Hi-Standard, Harrington & Richardson, and others turned their hands to this lucrative field. In addition, certain custom gunmakers are putting together Kentucky type long rifles, black powder match rifles and some

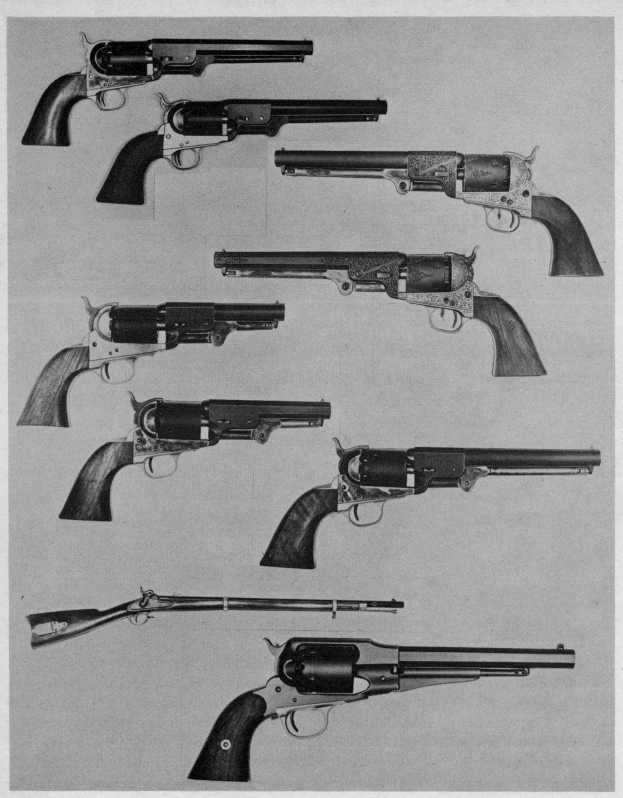

Reproductions of Colt, Remington and various Confederate caplock revolvers such as these, along with some vintage shoulder arms, have been manufactured abroad in recent years. While very popular with the black powder shooting clan, some have occasionally caused problems in identification for antique arms collectors.

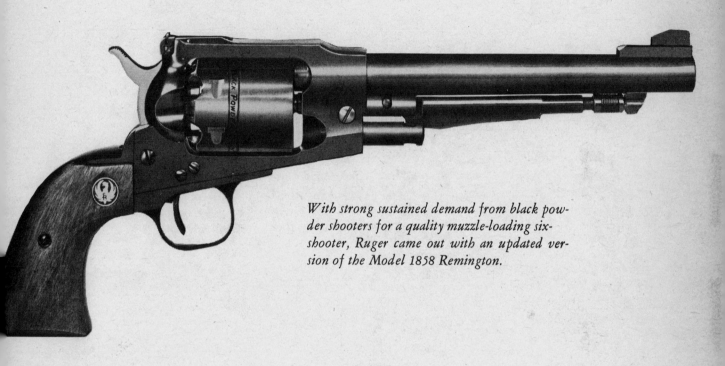

With strong sustained demand from black powder shooters for a quality muzzle-loading six-shooter, Ruger came out with an updated version of the Model 1858 Remington.

flintlock and caplock hunting guns equal in workmanship to those of the old masters. Black powder muzzle-loading matches have increased greatly in number and interest. The National Muzzle-loading Rifle Association has an active and enthusiastic membership.

There is significance in the current manufacture of such single-shots as the old Sharps Borchardt type, the Winchester "High Wall" and the Farquaharson type rifle, all made now by other than the original producers who long ago abandoned manufacture.

Few promotions have succeeded like the appeal to history and patriotism represented by the practice of offering inscribed "Commemorative" pistols, initiated by Colt. Started in 1961 with their 125th Anniversary Model S.A.A., Colt has now turned out countless differently inscribed pistols, usually boxed, and some in pairs, honoring places, events and important persons. It was too good a sales idea to ignore and soon many of the other manufacturers began offering "Commemorative" handguns and rifles of their own. The formation of a very active Commemorative Gun Collectors Association has resulted.

More attention is being given to pistols and and rifles shooting pellets and BB shot, either

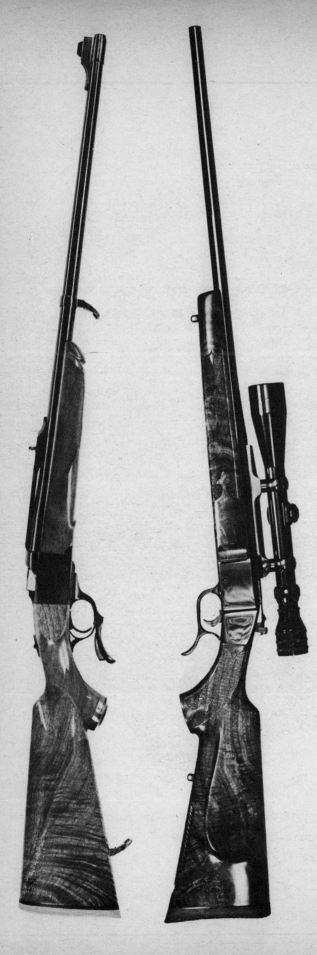

The burgeoning interest in muzzle-loaders has also sparked a parallel enthusiasm for quality single-shot cartridge rifles. The experimental Colt (right) has a dropping block action reminiscent of the Sharps, while the Ruger (on the left) is similar to the Farquaharson.

air or CO_2 propelled. Arms of this powderless type now are recognized in official matches. All in all, enthusiasm for all forms of shooting sports and with a great variety of arms has grown rapidly. In the National Rifle Association alone there are over a million members. Numerous gun collectors associations are spread across the country.

From the oldest to the latest, guns continue to arouse widespread interest. Whether a wealthy collector is moved to spend $5000 for a fine antique specimen or a young hunter just likes to get out in the woods with a $50 rifle, all have an interest in how their hobby

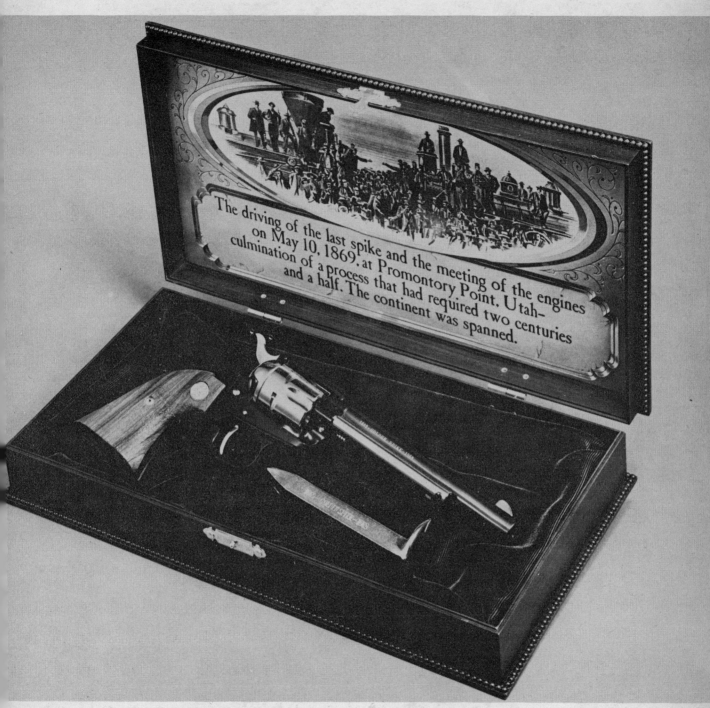

The driving of the last spike and the meeting of the engines on May 10, 1869, at Promontory Point, Utah— culmination of a process that had required two centuries and a half. The continent was spanned.

One of the most successful gun promotions of all times was the Colt initiated idea of "commemorative" models. Many historical events and personages have been honored and thousands of pistols sold, and the very active Colt Commemorative Gun Collectors Association of America formed. Several other manufacturers now produce commemorative models of their own.

Gun collectors are just as avid as target shooters and hunters in their enjoyment of their gun hobby. Shown here is a meeting of the Ohio Gun Collectors Association in Canton, Ohio several years ago. This group, probably the world's largest gun collectors organization, currently boasts over 8000 members and sees upwards of 5000 collectors from all over the world at each of its bi-monthly meetings.

or sport developed and what the history may be of those whose abilities and determination have made armsmaking one of the precise sciences.

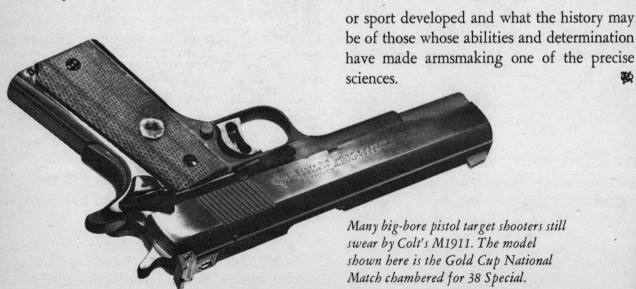

Many big-bore pistol target shooters still swear by Colt's M1911. The model shown here is the Gold Cup National Match chambered for 38 Special.

CHAPTER THIRTY-SIX

Arms in America — a Perspective

ew industries have shown the endurance of the armsmakers. Theirs has been a trade vital not only to the nation's recreational activities, but, in truth, to its very survival. Many of the pioneers in our three centuries of armsmaking have been forgotten, but the genius of a few has come down to us in well-documented records. Sometimes they risked much to promote their ideas and production. They saw good times and bad, but their progress was not to be stopped.

While it is obvious that the direction of businesses founded a century or more ago has changed, many of those original names—Colt,

Smith & Wesson continues to supply American shooters with quality arms after well over a century of service. This 41 Magnum Model 57 is very popular with hunters and law enforcement officers.

Hunting is often a family sport. This youngster's pride in knocking down this pheasant will be relived when he shares it with his family at the dinner table.

Despite the continuing popularity of older, well established models with America's shooters, new designs continue to be introduced. This all stainless steel 44 Auto Mag is the world's most powerful automatic pistol and has proved very popular with big game handgun hunters since its introduction several years ago.

Remington, Winchester, Smith & Wesson, Marlin, Savage, and others—are to be found on arms produced today. New respected names have been added to that illustrious list. It is a very competitive industry devoted to providing the tools best suited to the age-old sports of hunting and target shooting, to the needs of our country in maintaining an arsenal for our national defense, to equipping our law enforcement agencies, and to giving all Americans the means of greater security in their homes.

Those who would malign the armsmakers or demean those millions of our citizens who strongly believe in the right to own firearms, and use them in lawful pursuits, too conveniently forgot the role arms have played from earliest days in carving this nation out of a wilderness. They overlook the gun's role in the hard fought struggles to gain our independence and to replace tyranny with freedom and security. Changing times may require adjustments, but as the wise Bernard Baruch once said, "Everyone has a right to his opinions, but no one has a right to be wrong in his facts." The indisputable facts about guns and gunmakers in American life speak for themselves for those who wish to consider

Hunting is still one of America's favorite outdoor sports, and with their organized conservation efforts and license fees, hunters contribute the lion's share to preserving the nation's wildlife heritage.

them objectively. It is not claimed the record is spotless, but in light of the broad and important services this industry provides, and has provided in times of critical need, it certainly takes its place as one of our vital and indispensable national assets. Dedication to producing a useful, quality product, employed in lawful pursuits, has been the American armsmaker's primary goal. 🜚

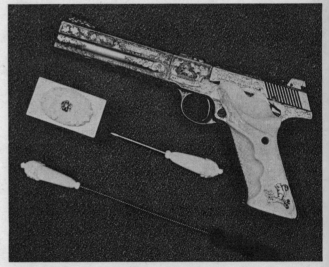

Whether he has them for utility, sport, collecting or the simple pleasure of possessing a fine art object such as this beautifully engraved Colt Match Target Woodsman, the American citizen has enjoyed the constitutionally protected right to keep and bear arms throughout the two centuries of our nation's existence.

Guns in America– a Chronological Outline

1492-3   Columbus lands in the West Indies, bringing the first firearms—cannon on his ships, and presumedly hand-carried wheel-locks and a matchlock—to the New World.

1500-1600   Spanish (and other) explorers bring the first firearms—"firesticks" to the natives—to the North American continent.

1630   Early American gunsmith, Eltweeed Pomeroy, opens a shop in Dorchester, Massachusetts Bay Colony.

1643   An iron works is established in Lynn, Massachusetts.

1646   Covert Barent opens a gunsmith shop in New Amsterdam (New York).

1685   A gunsmith, John Hawkins, opens shop at Charles Town, Carolina Colony.

1719   Pennsylvania or "Kentucky" rifles are made by Martin Meylin in Lancaster, Pennsylvania Colony.

1750   A nine shot flintlock rifle is constructed by John Cookson at Boston, Massachusetts Colony.

1776   Continental Congress establishes the name "United States" and provides that all government arms be marked "U. States" or "U.S." Congress also exempts all gun makers from military service.

1795 First official U.S. shoulder arm, the Model 1795 musket is adopted. Congress establishes Springfield Armory.

1796 Harper's Ferry (Virginia) Armory is authorized by President George Washington.

1797 The Virginia Manufactory is established in Richmond to make arms for the Virginia militia.

1798 Eli Whitney receives a government contract to make flintlock muskets in his Whitneyville, Connecticut plant.

1799 Simeon North receives a government contract for 500 flintlock pistols to be made at his works at Berlin, Connecticut.

1806 The U.S. Model 1806 pistol, first official U.S. designed martial handgun, is adopted. Henry Deringer goes into the gun business in Philadelphia.

1810 A revolving-cylinder flintlock pistol is developed by Elisha Collier in Boston, Massachusetts.

1811 Captain John Hall patents his breech-loading flintlock rifle. George Tryon establishes a gun shop in Philadelphia that is destined to become the nation's longest-lived gun distributing company.

1816 The copper percussion cap is developed by Joshua Shaw of Philadelphia. Eliphalet Remington founds his arms company in Ilion Gorge, New York.

1819 Hall's flintlock rifle becomes the first breech-loader to be adopted by the U.S. government.

1822 The Hawken brothers, later famous for their rugged, reliable "Rocky Mountain" rifles, go into business in St. Louis.

1825 Henry Deringer introduces his famous short-barreled large-bore pocket pistol.

1836 Samuel Colt is awarded a patent for his percussion revolver and founds the Patent Arms Manufacturing Company in Paterson, New Jersey.

1837 Ethan Allen patents the pepperbox.

1840 First U.S. martial percussion-cap fired arm, the Model 1840 carbine, is adopted.

1847 Colt develops his Walker model, the design upon which subsequent Colt revolvers will be based.

1848 A self-contained cartridge is patented by Walter Hunt. Sharps patents his breech-loading action.

1849 Rollin White patents the bored-through cylinder concept for revolvers.

1854 Horace Smith and Daniel Wesson patent the "Volcanic" pistol, which uses Hunt's cartridge.

1857 Oliver Winchester takes over Smith and Wesson's Volcanic Arms Company. Smith and Wesson market the first U.S. cartridge revolver, a compact 22.

1860 Winchester introduces the Henry rifle. Parker Snow & Company (later Parker Brothers) is founded by Charles Parker.

1861 The first Ballard rifles are made by Ball & Williams in Worcester, Massachusetts.

1862   A new government arsenal is established at Rock Island, Illinois.

1864   Joshua Stevens founds his gun company, later J. Stevens Arms & Tool Company.

1867   Union Metallic Cartridge Company (UMC) is established in Bridgeport, Connecticut.

1868   Hopkins & Allen is founded in Norwich, Connecticut. United States Cartridge Company begins operation in Lowell, Massachusetts.

1870   John Mahlon Marlin founds the Marlin Firearms Company in New Haven, Connecticut.

1871   The National Rifle Association is organized. Harrington & Richardson go into business.

1873   Colt introduces the Model 1873 Single Action Army pistol, Winchester the Model 1873 lever action rifle, and Springfield Armory the Model 1873 "trapdoor" rifle.

1874   A team of U.S. riflemen defeat the crack Irish rifle team at Creedmoor, Long Island.

1875   John Marlin acquires rights to the Ballard rifle action.

1876   Hugo Borchardt designs a swingout cylinder revolver for Winchester.

1879   John M. Browning of Ogden, Utah Territory patents his first single-shot rifle action.

1883   Browning begins his association with Winchester.

1884 Hiram Maxim patents a locked-breech semi-automatic rifle and Browning patents the design for the Winchester Model 1886 rifle.

1889 Colt markets the first commercial swingout cylinder revolver.

1892 The U.S. Army adopts the Norwegian-designed Krag-Jorgensen bolt-action repeating rifle.

1895 Colt produces the Browning-designed Model 1895 "potato digger" machine gun for the U.S. Army. Arthur W. Savage founds the Savage Arms Company in Utica, New York.

1897 Browning receives his first patents for self-loading pistol designs.

1900 Colt introduces the first U.S. automatic pistol, the Browning designed Model 1900. Browning patents his first automatic shotgun.

1901 The U.S. Army issues its first self-loading automatic pistols for field test, 200 Colt Model 1900s and 1000 Model 1900 Lugers.

1903 The Springfield Model 1903 bolt action rifle, a modification of the German Mauser, is adopted by the U.S. Army. Winchester introduces the first U.S. semi-auto rifle for commercial sale, the 22 caliber Model 1903.

1904 Rock Island (Illinois) arsenal begins production on the Model 1903 rifle.

1906 The first U.S. high powered semi-auto rifle, the Browning designed Remington Model 8, is put on the market.

1911 The U.S. Army adopts Colt's Browning designed Model 1911 45 caliber self-loading pistol.

1917 Browning demonstrates his semi-automatic rifle (the BAR) and heavy machine guns to the U.S. Army.

1921 The Thompson submachine gun, made by Colt for Auto-Ordnance Corporation, is put on the market.

1926 High Standard Corporation is founded.

1934 The National Firearms Act, which controls the ownership and transfer of machine guns, sawed-off shotguns and other "gangster-style" weapons, is passed.

1936 The U.S. Army adopts the Garand semi-automatic rifle and becomes the first major world power to adopt a self-loader as standard issue.

1941 The U.S. M1 carbine is developed by Winchester for issue to support troops.

1949 Sturm, Ruger & Company enter the gun field with a low-cost 22 auto pistol.

1954 Smith & Wesson announce the first U.S. double action high power semi-auto pistol, the Model 39.

1965 MB Associates introduces the Gyro Jet, a rocket firing self-loading pistol.

1968 The Gun Control Act of 1968, which severely restricts importation and interstate traffic in firearms is passed into law.

1976 As our nation enters its bicentennial anniversary the private ownership of guns—one of the issues important to our decision to fight for independence two centuries ago and a right which received Constitutional guarantee in the Bill of Rights—is under very strong attack from those who are naive enough to equate gun ownership with lawlessness.